Undertaking a health assessment

A guide to collecting and analysing health information using CoramBAAF's integrated health forms

Florence Merredew and Carolyn Sampeys

www.corambaaf.org.uk

Published by
CoramBAAF Adoption and Fostering Academy
41 Brunswick Square
London WC1N 1AZ
www.corambaaf.org.uk

Coram Academy Limited, registered as a company limited by guarantee in England and Wales number 9697712, part of the Coram group, charity number 312278

© CoramBAAF, 2017

British Library Cataloguing in Publication Data
A catalogue record for this book is available from the British Library

ISBN 978 1 910039 60 1

Designed and typeset by Helen Joubert Design Ltd
Printed in Great Britain by The Lavenham Press

All rights reserved. Apart from any fair dealing for the purposes of research or private study, or criticism or review, as permitted under the Copyright, Designs and Patents Act 1988, this publication may not be reproduced, stored in a retrieval system, or transmitted in any form or by any means, without the prior written permission of the publishers.

The moral right of the author has been asserted in accordance with the Copyright, Designs and Patents Act 1988.

Contents

1 How to use this guide — 1
Introduction — 1
What this guide is — 2
What this guide is not — 2
Why use CoramBAAF health forms? — 3

2 Legal issues and statutory duties for health assessments — 5
Health assessment on becoming looked after — 5
Review health assessment — 6
Health assessment for adoption — 6

3 Consent — 8
Who can give consent? — 8
Consent to access and share health information — 12
Court orders to carry out health assessments — 13

4 The initial health assessment — 16
The role of the social worker — 16
Comprehensive health assessment — 17
Obtaining initial information — 18
Engagement — 20
Who undertakes the initial health assessment? — 20
Consent Form: consent to obtain and share health information — 21
Form M: mother's health — 27
Form B: baby's health — 28
Form PH: report on health of birth parent — 30
Form IHA–C: initial health assessment for child from birth to nine years — 32
Form IHA–YP: initial health assessment for young person 10 years and older — 38

5 The review health assessment — 40
Form RHA–C: review health assessment for child from birth to nine years — 40
Form RHA–YP: review health assessment for young person 10 years and older — 45

6 Assessment of mental health and well-being — 48
Carers' reports — 48
Strengths and Difficulties Questionnaire (SDQ) — 49

7 Case examples — 51
Case 1: Birth mother with history of substance use — 51
Case 2: Birth mother with history of physical and mental health conditions — 56
Case 3: Birth father with learning difficulties and family history of heart disease — 58

8 Adult health assessment — 61
Purpose of the adult health assessment — 61
Legal and statutory duties — 62
Health reviews — 66
Form AH: adult health assessment process and documentation — 69
Interagency working between the medical adviser and social worker/agency — 72
Health review — 73
Form AH2: update adult health report — 73
Form AH Review — 75

9 Additional resources — 76

Bibliography — 77

Appendix: CoramBAAF health forms — 80

Notes about the authors

Florence Merredew was a GP and psychotherapist in Canada before moving to the UK and has worked as Health Consultant at BAAF (now CoramBAAF) since 2001. Her remit is to promote the health of looked after children and their carers through co-ordination of the CoramBAAF Health Group Advisory Committee, raising awareness, improving standards, and contributing to best practice and training.

Carolyn Sampeys is a community paediatrician and named doctor for adoption, fostering and looked after children for Cardiff and Vale University Health Board. She acts as medical adviser in adoption to Cardiff and Vale of Glamorgan local authorities. She is also designated doctor for safeguarding children within the National Safeguarding Team, Public Health Wales, with a particular remit for looked after children and adoption across Wales. Carolyn was instrumental in the development of the role of the specialist looked after children nurse in Wales and has contributed to several consultations and changes in regulations relating to looked after children and adoption. She represents the NHS on the Wales National Adoption Service Advisory Group, and the National Fostering Framework Strategic Steering Group. She is a past Chair of the BAAF Cymru Health Group and was elected Chair of the BAAF (now CoramBAAF) UK Health Group Advisory Committee in 2010.

Acknowledgements

Although there are two authors named on the cover, this book rests on the foundation created by those dedicated health professionals who developed the suite of revised child health assessment forms detailed in this guide. Over a series of meetings and revisions, they contributed their professional experience and knowledge in a range of specialist areas, ensuring that the forms address the complex and diverse needs of looked after children and young people, including those with an adoption plan. We offer our heartfelt thanks to the working group: Anne Akamo, Melanie Bracewell, Kath Burton, Gita Croft, Lin Graham-Ray, Efun Johnson and also to Jean Burbidge, Marie Davies and Jackie Keegan who attended one lengthy meeting to bring not just their own perspectives but the collective wisdom of other specialist nurses. In addition, thanks to the many medical advisers and specialist nurses who fed back on the forms over the years and during consultation.

Health practice in fostering and adoption is embedded within a statutory framework and neither the forms nor this guide would have been completed without the assistance of various CoramBAAF (previously BAAF), AFA Cymru and AFA Scotland colleagues. We extend much appreciation to Alexandra Conroy Harris and Leonie Jordan, Priscilla McLoughlin, Sarah Coldrick and Alexandra Plumtree, who provided legal advice on the forms and guidebook for England, Northern Ireland, Wales and Scotland respectively. Paul Adams and Jacqui Lawrence, Fostering Consultants, and Elaine Dibben, Adoption Consultant, answered queries about best practice in social care. Danielle Sawyer provided administrative support and John Simmonds was an ongoing source of expertise. Finally, thanks to Shaila Shah and Jo Francis in CoramBAAF Publications for their help.

How to use this guide

Introduction

Health professionals with expertise in the health issues and needs of looked after children (LAC) and their carers, and in fostering and adoption issues, have developed the CoramBAAF integrated health forms. The forms promote a quality standard in obtaining health information on birth parents and assessing the health needs of looked after children, including those with a plan for adoption, and assessing carers and adopters. This essential information is crucial to ensuring that a child/young person's health needs are addressed in their placement with substitute carers, and that essential family health information is recorded and accompanies the child or young person into adulthood.

The CoramBAAF forms are intended to complement each other and enable the appropriate sharing of relevant health information in the best interests of the child or young person concerned. The initial health assessment (IHA) and review health assessment (RHA) forms enable a comprehensive, holistic health assessment, fulfilling statutory requirements across the UK. Together with information obtained from parental health (PH), mother (M) and baby (B) forms, with the accompanying consent (Consent Form), the IHA/RHA forms enable the collation of information and interpretation by the health professional in a format to share with multi-agency colleagues, allowing for confidentiality and consent considerations.

The CoramBAAF forms promote and are reliant upon multidisciplinary and interagency working. Social workers have a role in providing demographic details, current circumstances and background information. They also have an important task in supporting birth parents in completing the consent and parental health forms.

Although the agency health adviser or medical adviser is required to collate the available information, the midwife, neonatal team, health visitor, school nurse, GP and examining health professional all have important roles in gathering the health information.

The social worker is then required to formulate the Health Care Plan using the health recommendations and to take action where necessary. The Independent Reviewing Officer (IRO)/reviewing officer will ensure that the health assessment and health recommendations are considered at the time of the LAC Review.

UNDERTAKING A HEALTH ASSESSMENT

What this guide is

This guide will help professionals understand the importance of their individual roles and responsibilities in completing health assessments. It explains why the information is required, how and when it should be collected and with whom it should be shared. It explores consent requirements, confidentiality and information sharing, and provides examples of good practice on the use of the forms.

The guide addresses the legislative framework and requirements to assess the health of looked after children in England, Northern Ireland, Scotland and Wales, and outlines what is needed for adoption. It discusses in detail the central issue of obtaining informed consent to access health information, to carry out the health assessment and subsequently to share health information within the social care context. The initial health assessment is then addressed, followed by detailed guidance on the use of the relevant forms. The review health assessment process and relevant forms are discussed next, followed by consideration of mental health.

The children's health assessment forms have been designed for flexible use. To assist the health professional carrying out the assessment, the IHA and RHA forms contain many prompts about possible relevant considerations for each section; however, the assessor should consider what is appropriate for each child. The health professional assessing the child must consider the collated information concerning individual and family health history and analyse its impact on current and future health in order to formulate a summary and recommendations for the child care plan. This guide aids the process of consideration and analysis of this material.

The principles in approaching adult health assessment are also explored in this guide, followed by detailed guidance on completion of each form. Crucially, the medical adviser must analyse the information, obtain further information if needed, and provide a summary of health risk for consideration by the panel, agency decision-maker and at matching.

Throughout the guide, the emphasis is on obtaining comprehensive health information on both looked after children and prospective carers, and subsequently analysing this information to understand current health and the implications for future health, to contribute to planning in the best interests of children. We hope that this guide will be a useful tool in multidisciplinary training.

What this guide is not

This guide is not intended to be a quick and easy way of undertaking health assessments. It offers a way of understanding the different forms in use, and the purpose and contribution of each to formulating a high quality assessment of the child's health needs, and health risk of adult carers. It highlights the roles of the social worker and health professional and provides detailed guidance on best practice relevant to completing each section, and facilitates the crucial step of analysing health information.

How to use this guide

The guide should be seen as a tool to help in the health assessment process and not as an end in itself.

Why use CoramBAAF health forms?

The use of the CoramBAAF health forms is advisable because:

- the integrated suite of forms fulfils the primary purpose of the statutory health assessment of the looked after child to provide a child-centred comprehensive assessment;
- they collate important health information for children and their families;
- they provide a standardised method for collecting information on children who could otherwise lose health information about themselves and their families;
- use of a standardised form throughout the UK promotes the same good practice and facilitates placement across borders;
- the forms are compliant with regulations and guidance throughout the UK;
- the forms are designed by agency medical advisers, paediatricians and specialist nurses in consultation with legal advisers, are reviewed by the CoramBAAF Health Group in accordance with changes in Government guidance and subsequent practice, and have undergone extensive consultation with practitioners across the UK;
- the forms provide a UK-wide standardised basis for assessing carers in relation to their ability to care for vulnerable children. With the frequency of interagency placements and consortia, and the establishment of regional adoption agencies (RAAs) in England and the National Adoption Service in Wales, having standardised assessments has become increasingly important.

The complete system of integrated CoramBAAF children's health assessment forms includes:

- Consent Form (consent for obtaining and sharing health information)
- Form M (mother's health)
- Form B (baby's health)
- Form PH (parental health)
- Form IHA–C (initial health assessment for child from birth to nine years)
- Form IHA–YP (initial health assessment for young person 10 years and older)
- Form RHA–C (review health assessment for child from birth to nine years)
- Form RHA–YP (review health assessment for young person 10 years and older)
- Form CR–C (carers' report – profile of behavioural and emotional well-being of child from birth to nine years)

UNDERTAKING A HEALTH ASSESSMENT

- Form CR–YP (carers' report – profile of behavioural and emotional well-being of young person aged 10–16 years)

There are two CoramBAAF forms to assess adult health:

- Form AH (initial comprehensive adult health assessment of applicants)
- Form AH2 (update of Form AH)

Legal issues and statutory duties for health assessments

2

There are various legal and statutory duties for health assessments of looked after children, in the different UK countries.

Health assessment on becoming looked after

Regulations throughout the UK* require the local authority to ensure that arrangements are made for a child to have a comprehensive health assessment carried out prior to or shortly after placement. The local authority must obtain from the practitioner a written assessment of the child's state of health and health care needs. In England and Northern Ireland, this assessment must be carried out by a registered medical practitioner, whereas in Wales a registered nurse with appropriate skills can carry out the assessment if this is considered by the looked after children health team to best meet the needs of the child or children. In Scotland, the assessment may be carried out by either a registered medical practitioner or a registered nurse.

In England, the Statutory Guidance *Promoting the Health and Well-Being of Looked After Children* (DfE and DH, 2015) states that:

> *The initial health assessment should result in a health plan, which is available in time for the first statutory review by the Independent Reviewing Officer (IRO) of the child's care plan. That case review must happen within 20 working days from when the child started to be looked after.*

In Wales, the Care Planning, Placement and Case Review (Wales) Regulations 2015 state that:

> *Before a child is placed or, if that is not reasonably practicable, before the first review of the child's case, the responsible authority must make arrangements for a registered medical practitioner or registered nurse to:*

---

* Regulation 7 of the Care Planning, Placement and Case Review (England) Regulations 2010, regulation 7 of the Care Planning, Placement and Case Review (Wales) Regulations 2015, regulation 7 of the Arrangements for Placement of Children (General) Regulations (Northern Ireland) 1996 and regulation 3(3)(b) of the Looked After Children (Scotland) Regulations 2009.

- *Carry out a health assessment unless an assessment has been carried out within the preceding three months;*
- *Provide a written report of the assessment as soon as reasonably practicable.*

In Northern Ireland, the Arrangements for Placement of Children (General) Regulations (Northern Ireland) 1996 require Trusts to arrange for a child to be medically examined by a doctor who is required to compile a written report on the child's health, prior to a placement being made, or, where this is not possible, as soon as practical after placement.

In Scotland, the Looked After Children (Scotland) Regulations 2009 require the local authority 'to obtain a written assessment of the child's health and their need for health care by a registered medical practitioner or registered nurse' (regulation 3(3)(b)). The local authority must obtain a wide range of information about the child (regulation 3(3)(a)) and make a full assessment of the child's needs (regulations 3(2)(a) and 4(1)). This assessment includes information about the child's existing health arrangements and whether these need to be changed (regulation 4(1)(i)). Following the assessment, a 'child's plan' is prepared (regulation 5), and must include the health assessment (regulation 5(3)(e)).

The medical examination and assessment are not required if they have already been carried out in the three months immediately preceding the date on which the child began to be looked after by the local authority. However, even when this is the case, there may well be circumstances in which the child's history or current presentation warrant further comprehensive examination or assessment. This will be a matter for individual clinical judgement.

Review health assessment

In England, Wales and Northern Ireland, regulations and guidance require a review health assessment every six months until the child's fifth birthday, and then every 12 months thereafter (Care Planning, Placement and Case Review (England) Regulations 2010; Care Planning, Placement and Case Review (Wales) Regulations 2015, *Children (Northern Ireland) Order 1995 Guidance and Regulations Volume 3: Family Placements and Private Fostering*. **In Scotland**, the regulations do not specifically refer to review health assessments. However, the provisions for each review of the child's care require further ongoing assessment of all aspects of the child's needs, welfare and development, and the revision of the child's plan. Ongoing medical assessment of the child must therefore be undertaken as a crucial part of this work (Looked After Children (Scotland) Regulations 2009, regulations 44 and 45).

Health assessment for adoption

Adoption regulations recognise the importance of the medical contribution in the context of adoption and every adoption agency is required to make arrangements for the appointment of at least one medical practitioner to be the agency's medical adviser. Details of this role are described in regulations for each country and in Merredew and Sampeys, 2015.

Regulations in **England, Wales and Northern Ireland** require that the agency medical adviser provide a summary of the child's health, including health history, and any need for future health care, to be included in the Child's Permanence Report (Form CPR) in England, Child's Adoption Report (Form CAR) in Wales and Child's Adoption Report NI (Form CAR-NI) in Northern Ireland. The matters to be included in the health report are specified in the Regulations (Adoption Agencies Regulations 2005, Adoption Agencies (Wales) Regulations 2005 and Adoption Agencies (Northern Ireland) Regulations 1989. If the child is looked after, then this report may be based on the statutory health assessments that have already been undertaken.

When the agency is considering adoption for a looked after child, they should consult with the medical adviser to determine whether the information obtained from statutory health assessments that have already been undertaken is sufficiently comprehensive and up to date to provide the information needed by the agency decision-maker, matching panel and prospective adopters. If not, then timely arrangements for a new health assessment should be made to avoid unnecessary delay.

In Scotland, regulation 12(2)(d) and (e) of the Adoption Agencies (Scotland) Regulations 2009 requires that arrangements are made for a medical examination followed by a written assessment of the child's health. This medical report must be provided to any subsequent adoption panel for the child (regulation 12(4)(a)). The Child Adoption and Permanence Report (CAPR) must include the medical report and assessment.

3 Consent

Health professionals must have informed consent to undertake a health assessment. It is important to note that consent for two different purposes and activities must be considered here.

1. **Consent to access and share health information**. In order to complete a comprehensive and holistic health assessment and health care plan for a child, it may be necessary to access the child's and birth parents' health records, or to contact the relevant health professional. Informed consent is needed to obtain health information from these sources. Once the assessment and health care plan are formulated, it is often necessary to share the information with other health professionals, social workers and others planning the care, and with carers.

   The Consent Form is used for this purpose. A signed CoramBAAF Consent Form should accompany the request to complete Forms M, B, PH, IHA–C, IHA–YP, RHA–C and RHA–YP to facilitate access to additional child or family health information.

2. **Consent to health assessment, including examination**. The second activity requiring consent is the health assessment, which includes a discussion and possibly a physical examination, followed by the formulation of a health care plan. There is a section to be signed on each of the IHA and RHA health assessment forms indicating consent to carry out the assessment.

Who can give consent?

A child or young person may be able to give consent themselves, or there may be more than one adult who is able to give consent if they have parental responsibility/ies for that child. It is only necessary to obtain consent from one source, although it is good practice to consult all parties with parental responsibility/ies for a child. A court may also order an assessment or examination of a child. In addition, in Scotland, the children's hearing may make a medical examination order or include a medical measure in a compulsory supervision order or an interim compulsory supervision order.

Child with capacity to consent

In England and Wales, a child may consent to accessing and sharing their own health information and to assessment or treatment if they are thought to be competent to do so; that is, that they have sufficient maturity and understanding to consider the options and implications. A young person of 16 has the right to give consent to a medical assessment and treatment, but this may be rebutted if the young person has learning difficulties or is otherwise unable to understand the implications of consenting to an assessment or treatment (s.8, Family Law Reform Act 1969). The tests for deciding a child's competence were laid down in *Gillick v West Norfolk & Wisbech Area Health Authority* [1985] UKHL 7, as a result of which a child is now referred to as being "Gillick competent" or not. The case was brought by a mother who wanted assurances that her daughter would not be given contraception without the mother's knowledge and consent. The judgement of Lord Fraser gave specific guidelines on the prescribing of contraception to under-age girls without parental consent; these are known as the Fraser Guidelines. The principles set out have implications for all treatment of children, not just for the provision of contraception.

> ### Gillick competence
>
> *Parental right yields to the child's right to make his own decisions when he reaches a sufficient understanding and intelligence to be capable of making up his own mind on the matter requiring decision.*
>
> *...it is not enough that she should understand the nature of the advice which is being given: she must also have a sufficient maturity to understand what is involved.*
>
> Lord Scarman

In Scotland, consent to medical treatment, etc, must come from the child or young person aged under 16 when the medical practitioner considers that he or she has the capacity to understand the nature and consequences of the treatment, etc. This is set out in s.2(4) of the Age of Legal Capacity (Scotland) Act 1991. Parental consent is not required and cannot override the consent or non-consent of the capable child or young person, although it is good practice to seek parental consent as well, if possible. Only if the child or young person is considered unable to understand the nature and consequences of the treatment should consent be sought from a person with parental responsibilities.

In Scotland, the age of full capacity to consent to medical treatment, etc, is 16. If the young person is aged 16 or over, it is for him or her to consent. If he or she is not capable of consenting, the matter is dealt with as for any other incapable adult.

Parental responsibility in England, Wales and Northern Ireland

A woman who gives birth to a child automatically has parental responsibility for her child, which cannot be removed except by the child's adoption or, in the case of a surrogate mother, by parental order.

A father has parental responsibility if:

- he was married to the child's mother at the time of the child's birth, or has subsequently married her;
- he is named on the child's birth certificate (but only if the birth was registered on or after 15 April 2002 in Northern Ireland, or after 1 December 2003 in England and Wales);
- he has entered into a parental responsibility agreement with the child's mother; or
- a court has made a parental responsibility order in his favour.

Parental responsibility granted by a court may be removed by court order.

Parental responsibilities and rights in Scotland

A woman who gives birth to a child automatically has parental responsibilities and rights for her child. These cannot be removed except by a court order, including an adoption order or, in the case of a surrogate mother, by parental order.

A father has parental responsibilities and rights if:

- he was married to the child's mother at any time from the child's conception or subsequently;
- he is named on the child's birth certificate (but only if the birth was registered on or after 4 May 2006);
- he has entered into a parental responsibilities and rights agreement with the child's mother;
- he has been awarded some or all parental responsibilities and rights under a court order, including a residence/section 11 order; or
- the mother has died and has named him in her will as the person to have them on her death.

Parental responsibilities and/or rights granted by a court may be removed by a court.

Other ways to acquire parental responsibility/ies

Throughout the UK, adoptive parents of a child have parental responsibility/ies for that child from the date of the adoption order. Prospective adopters in England and Wales will have parental responsibility for a child placed with them for adoption, but such responsibility is subject to any restrictions imposed by the placing authority. In Northern Ireland and Scotland, adoptive parents acquire parental responsibility/ies only on the granting of an adoption order.

Where a child is conceived in a surrogacy arrangement, the commissioning parents will obtain parental responsibility/ies through a parental order, which allows for the re-registration of the child's birth naming them as the child's parents.

The female partner of a woman conceiving by artificial insemination will be able to register as a child's second female parent and so acquire parental responsibility/ies.

Consent

A step-parent (a person married to, or the civil partner of, a child's parent) may acquire parental responsibility/ies by court order or by adoption. In England, Wales and Northern Ireland, a step-parent may also acquire parental responsibility by a parental responsibility agreement.

In England and Wales, a person who is named in a court order as a special guardian for a child, or a person named as the person with whom the child should live under a residence order or child arrangements order (formerly a residence order till April 2014) has been made, has parental responsibility for that child for so long as the order remains in force. In England and Wales, a court must give a parent, and may give any other person named in a child arrangements order, parental responsibility. In Scotland, a person who has a residence order for a child under s.11 of the Children (Scotland) Act 1995 acquires parental responsibilities, unless he or she already has them.

A local authority in England and Wales or a Trust in Northern Ireland will have parental responsibility for a child under an emergency protection order or care order (interim or final). In England and Wales, it may also have parental responsibility through a placement order or, in Northern Ireland, a freeing order. The local authority/Trust will not have parental responsibility for a child who:

- is being cared for by it under a child assessment order; is under police protection;
- has been remanded into its care by a criminal court; or
- is being looked after in England under s.20 of the Children Act 1989 (with parental consent), in Wales under s.76 of the Social Services and Well-being Act 2014 (with parental consent), or in Northern Ireland under s.21 of the Children (Northern Ireland) Order 1995.

In Scotland, local authorities do not have any parental responsibilities and/or rights for a looked after child, unless there is a permanence order. So they have no parental responsibilities and/or rights for a child who is:

- accommodated under s.25 of the Children (Scotland) Act 1995 ("voluntary" care);
- the subject of a child protection or child assessment order; or
- the subject of a compulsory supervision order or interim compulsory supervision order.

Local authorities/Trusts, foster carers, private foster carers, relatives, childminders and others will not usually have parental responsibility/ies for a child but may be able to exercise another's parental responsibility/ies on their behalf. This is likely to be evidenced by written agreement (for instance, a placement agreement for foster carers). This is called "delegated authority" and may be given for a particular event or arrangement, e.g. a medical appointment.

In Scotland, foster or kinship carers for a child for whom there is a permanence order may have some parental responsibilities, possibly including the responsibility and right to consent or not consent to medical treatment, etc.

A medical professional will only require consent from one person with parental responsibility/ies. However, it is best practice to seek consent from all parties with parental responsibility/ies wherever feasible. If there is opposition to the treatment, there may be an application to court for a specific issue order or, in England, Wales and Northern Ireland, for directions under an interim care order or to the High Court for wardship. These orders have been used where one parent opposes immunisations, as well as in extreme cases where one party wishes to give or withhold lifesaving treatment.

Consent to access and share health information

A person's health records are treated as "sensitive personal information" under the Data Protection Act (DPA) 1998. They should usually only be disclosed where the subject of that information has consented to them being shared with others. If a person is capable of consenting or not consenting to medical treatment, etc, he or she will normally be the person who consents or does not consent to sharing it.

Child's records

A child who is capable of consenting or not consenting to medical treatment, etc, will need to be asked to give consent for disclosure of health information. If the child is not capable of consenting to the assessment and consent is given by a person with parental responsibility/ies for him or her, consent for disclosure of a child's health records may also be given by any person with parental responsibility/ies.

In England, Wales and Northern Ireland, the age at which a child is assumed to have capacity to consent to information sharing is 12, and the Department for Education has published guidance (2011).

In Scotland, capacity to consent to sharing information follows capacity to consent to medical treatment, etc. A child or young person's rights under the DPA 1998 are governed by s.66 of the Act. If he or she is 12 or over, he or she is presumed to have the capacity to consent. However, this does not exclude a child under 12 having the same rights, if he or she has capacity. Practitioners in Scotland should consult Plumtree, 2014.

Parent's records

If a parent refuses to consent to sharing their own medical records, it may still be possible to obtain relevant information. Information held on the mother's records may also be the child's information, to which they would be entitled under DPA principles, so, for example, a mother may refuse to allow disclosure about her substance use during pregnancy, but information that the foetus failed to gain an appropriate birth weight because of maternal smoking is the child's information and so can be shared. It will be for the data controller of the hospital or practice that holds the mother's notes to separate out the child's information from the mother's and decide what can be disclosed. Information about genetic conditions, conditions that could have been transmitted from mother to child during pregnancy, and infectious diseases to which the child could have been exposed while living with that parent may be disclosed if it is in the public interest to do so. Government guidance sets out helpful principles (HM Government, 2015); it refers to legislation, etc, for England, but the DPA 1998 applies across the UK, so the guidance is helpful to practitioners in all four countries. It may be in the public interest to disclose such information to enable testing or treatment that would protect the child from serious harm, notwithstanding the parent's refusal to consent. Legal advice or advice from your

Consent

organisation's Caldicott Guardian* should be sought before disclosing material in the public interest.

In Scotland, the Adoption (Disclosure of Information and Medical Information about Natural Parents) (Scotland) Regulations 2009, SSI 2009/268, may be helpful in obtaining certain medical information about the child's family if adoption is the plan for the child. Regulation 11 states that where the agency has not been able to obtain information about whether there is 'any history of genetically transmissible or other significant disease' in the birth mother's or father's families, a medical practitioner, such as a birth parent's GP, must disclose such information to the adoption agency on request.

If a parent has died, access to their medical records is governed in England, Wales and Scotland by the Access to Health Records Act 1990, and in Northern Ireland by the Access to Health Records (NI) Order 1993. This allows access to records by the personal representative (the executor of their will or the person to whom a grant of letters of administration has been made if the deceased died intestate in England, Wales or Northern Ireland) of the deceased person, who may not necessarily be their next of kin, or any person who may have a claim as a result of their death (which their child may have) to any information that would support their claim. Disclosure of a deceased person's records may also be made in the public interest in the same circumstance as where consent to disclosure is refused.

As a general rule, the requirements for consent to share a looked after child's health information for the purpose of health provision or care planning are the same as the consent to assessment; however, careful consideration must be given to disclosure of third party information, for example, to prospective carers. Only information that is relevant for the purpose should be shared and only with those who need to know.

Court orders to carry out health assessments

In the following situations, a health assessment may be directed by the court, which has the power to make detailed provision about the type and terms of any assessment, including where it will take place.

Section 43 of the Children Act 1989 (England and Wales) and Article 62 of the Children (Northern Ireland) Order 1995

If a local authority/Trust has reasonable cause to suspect that a child is suffering, or is likely to suffer, significant harm, they may apply for a child assessment order under s.43 of the Children Act 1989 or Article 62 of the Children (Northern Ireland) Order 1995, which compels a person having care of the child to produce the child for examination as directed and gives the medical practitioner authority to carry out the assessment ordered, notwithstanding the lack of parental consent. A fully informed and competent child may refuse such an assessment.

---

* Organisations that access patient records are required to have a Caldicott Guardian, who is a senior person responsible for protecting the confidentiality of patients and service user information, and enabling appropriate information sharing.

Section 38 of the Children Act 1989 (England and Wales) and Article 57 of the Children (Northern Ireland) Order 1995

Where a court makes an interim care or interim supervision order, it may make an order for medical, psychiatric or other assessment of the child, that will not require parental consent, although the child may refuse the assessment if of sufficient understanding to make an informed decision. A court may also make an order that no, or no particular type of, assessment of a child shall take place. This provision was introduced as a result of the Cleveland Inquiry, where 125 children were subjected to testing for sexual abuse by one paediatrician.

Orders for health examinations and assessments: Scotland

In Scotland, a Children's Hearing may make a medical examination order (MEO) under the Children's Hearings (Scotland) Act 2011. It may also include a "measure" (condition) about medical treatment, etc, in a compulsory supervision order or interim compulsory supervision order. A sheriff may make a child protection or child assessment order under the 2011 Act and these orders may include provisions about medical examination, etc.

Any such order or provision under the 2011 Act overrides parental refusal to consent, but does not override the capable child's consent or non-consent (s.186).

It is also possible in theory for a court to make a specific issue order under s.11 of the Children (Scotland) Act 1995, dealing with medical matters for a child, but few if any such applications have been made. A local authority cannot make an application for any order under s.11.

Duty to arrange a health assessment

In England, Wales and Northern Ireland, consent is not required where a local authority has a duty to arrange a health assessment of a child.* A medical practitioner's authority to carry out an assessment is derived from the local authority's request each time a health assessment is undertaken, and the local authority can document this on CoramBAAF's Forms IHA–C/IHA–YP and RHA–C/RHA–YP.

It is important to note that although this duty does not provide consent to access health records, the report of the assessment must be submitted to the review and considered, and so will be shared with the child, social worker, Independent Reviewing Officer, foster carer, adoptive parents, etc, as part of the review. However, the provisions that impose the duty to carry out an assessment also provide an exception to the duty if the child refuses to consent, 'being of sufficient age and understanding to do so' (regulation 7(4) in England, regulation 7(4) in Wales, and regulation 7(B) in Northern Ireland. However, it is still good practice for local authorities to seek child and/or parental consent for a health assessment, particularly when a child is admitted to voluntary accommodation.

In Scotland, local authorities do not have parental responsibilities and rights for looked after children, unless there is a permanence order. As a result, they cannot provide implicit consent for health examinations and assessments unless there is a permanence

---

* For example, a looked after child's medical under regulation 7 of the Care Planning, Placement and Case Review (England) Regulations 2010, regulation 7 of the Care Planning, Placement and Case Review (Wales) Regulations 2015 or regulation 7 of the Arrangements for Placement of Children (General) Regulations (Northern Ireland) 1996.

order. Consent may be obtained from the child if capable of consenting, and if not, from a person with parental responsibilities. Consent is not needed if there is a medical examination order or similar from a children's hearing, or a court order such as a child protection order with a medical examination condition. However, none of these can override a capable child's right to refuse to consent.

4 The initial health assessment

Information concerning the child's antenatal, birth and health history and family history is required to complete a comprehensive initial health assessment. Consent must be obtained to access this information. Completion of the following forms will ensure that all necessary health and social information is obtained for the initial health assessment and care plan:

- Consent Form (consent for obtaining and sharing of health information)
- Form M (mother's health)
- Form B (baby's health)
- Form PH (parental health)
- Form IHA–C (initial health assessment for child from birth to nine years) or
- Form IHA–YP (initial health assessment for young person 10 years and older)

The role of the social worker

The social care agency has an important role to play in facilitating the initial health assessment. They should ensure that there is an effective system in place to notify the looked after children health team immediately when a child comes into care, so that an appointment can be made for a timely initial assessment resulting in a health care plan or child's plan. In England and Wales, this plan is required within 20 working days, as specified in regulations and guidance. Information regarding any concerns about personal safety of anyone involved **must** be shared at this point. The social worker should also help prepare the child for this initial health assessment, by explaining its purpose and what will happen at the appointment; some agencies have a leaflet that can be given to the child. Arrangements should be made for the social worker, foster carer and birth parents to attend the health assessment, unless this is contraindicated due to safeguarding issues. This is particularly helpful for obtaining the complete health history of the child and his or her parents, as well as building a co-operative working relationship with the family to address health inequalities and to promote the child's health and well-being.

The social worker should ensure that arrangements are made for an interpreter or signer to be present if necessary.

It is the responsibility of the social worker to either obtain the birth parent's consent to undertake a health assessment (documented on Form IHA), or to document that such consent has been given as part of the paperwork arranging for the child to become looked after. It is also the responsibility of the social worker to ask the birth parents to sign the CoramBAAF Consent Form so that health histories of the child and family may be accessed, and shared at a later point when required. The social worker should also ask each birth parent to provide their health history by completing Form PH (parental health), offering assistance if needed. In Northern Ireland, the birth parents are also asked to consent to their GP completing the Adopt 3B Birth Family History Information (Adoption Regional Policy and Procedures, 2010). Additionally, by completing Part A of Form IHA, which provides information on the child's social history, legal status and reason for coming into care, the social worker ensures that the health practitioner has important details about the child.

Comprehensive health assessment

Practice surrounding the health assessment of looked after children varies across the UK. In light of the significant health inequalities experienced by most looked after children, we believe it is essential for best practice, and Government guidance supports the principle that all looked after children should have a comprehensive health assessment carried out shortly after entering care. Regardless of their ultimate pathway through care, all looked after children deserve a comprehensive assessment of their health and development, as appropriate for their age. The following should all be undertaken:

- antenatal and birth history and early developmental history;
- family history;
- past medical history, including experiences of abuse and neglect and a chronological list of health events, including injuries and common illnesses;
- current physical health;
- sexual health and lifestyle issues, as appropriate for their age;
- mental health and behaviour, including experiences of trauma and loss;
- due to the high prevalence of mental health problems, a Carers' Report and Strength and Difficulties Questionnaire (SDQ) should be obtained;
- physical examination;
- developmental and functional assessment;
- health promotion, as appropriate for the child's age.

The initial health assessment creates an opportunity to get to know the child and, for older children and young people, to discuss their health concerns. The emphasis should be on engaging the young person in the assessment, as an initial step towards working in

UNDERTAKING A HEALTH ASSESSMENT

partnership and assisting them over time to assume responsibility for their own health. To the extent that it is appropriate for the child's maturity and understanding, the issues raised in the initial health assessment should be discussed with the child.

Obtaining initial information

We cannot emphasise too strongly the importance of obtaining as much information as possible when it first appears probable that a child will be looked after. This may be the only chance to obtain early health information and a family history, as it is impossible to foretell how long children will be in care or accommodation, or whether contact with birth relatives will continue in the future. Early knowledge is essential to the provision of current health care, as well as in planning long-term placements for children and in helping carers and adoptive parents to deal with health problems that may occur later.

We also know that adults who were separated from their birth families in early childhood often become anxious about their own or their children's health when they do not have access to their early health history.

It is therefore extremely important for both social workers and health professionals to engage effectively with the child's birth parents at the time of the initial health assessment. As well as accessing child and family health information, the assessment serves to raise awareness of health inequalities and issues with the birth parents that will need to be addressed if the child returns home. Social workers have a crucial role to play in obtaining and sharing information about parental lifestyles and the family's social history with health professionals. Having early knowledge of issues such as parental substance use and domestic violence assists the health professional to consider risk factors for physical and mental health conditions, and arrange screening, referral and interventions when appropriate.

At times, it may be necessary to obtain further health information about a sibling who is not looked after, for example, one with a genetic condition. It will be important to identify who can give consent to access such information.

Social care records, including psychology and independent expert reports, may at times reveal potentially important but undocumented information about the health of family members. It is important to record such information as "hearsay" and, wherever possible, to obtain consent to access accurate data.

The high incidence of mental health needs in the looked after children population is well recognised (Meltzer *et al*, 2003). In addition to the significant trauma experienced by many children before becoming looked after, the care system presents further challenges, with changes in living arrangements, frequent moves and placement breakdown. The importance of gathering information and reports to help identify emotional and behavioural disorders and other mental health problems cannot be underestimated. CoramBAAF's Carers' Report can be a useful tool, particularly for younger children. Many professionals have included screening tools like the Strengths and Difficulties Questionnaire (SDQ) (Goodman, 1997) to help with assessment of children from four to 16 years of age. These tools are discussed in more detail in Chapter 6 on mental health and well-being. For a comprehensive discussion of mental health and well-being, see Merredew and Sampeys, 2015, Chapter 4.

It is also important to obtain information about the ethnic and cultural background, language and religion of the child's birth family, as these will have relevance to the health and well-being of the child. Knowledge of a child's ethnic background can assist with appropriate screening for certain hereditary conditions that are prevalent in particular ethnic groups, for example, sickle cell anaemia, thalassaemia and Tay-Sachs disease.

Much additional information is required to understand the health needs of refugee and trafficked children, who have frequently had experiences beyond the norm for children raised in the UK. It is essential to consider the impact on their health of their country of origin and route taken, experiences en route, entry point into the UK, infectious diseases, the impact of displacement, separation and loss, physical, emotional and sexual trauma, sexual health and mental health.

Additionally, there is evidence that it is usually in the child's best interests to be in a placement that can reflect as fully as possible their ethnic and cultural background, language and religion. This becomes especially important for children who remain in care in the long term, or for whom a permanent placement is sought, who may experience confusion about their identity, with adverse effects on their self-esteem and emotional health and well-being.

However, **in England** the Department for Education has made it clear in Adoption Statutory Guidance (July 2013 revision, Chapter 4), that delay in permanent placements while waiting for a "perfect match" regarding ethnicity, language and culture is unacceptable. The statutory requirement for adoption agencies to give due consideration to religion, race and cultural background was removed for placements in England by the Children and Families Act 2014, but remains a requirement in Wales.

In Scotland, local authorities, adoption agencies and courts have duties to consider a child's 'religious persuasion, racial origin and cultural and linguistic background' in a range of decisions. Medical advisers and other registered medical practitioners and nurses must bear these duties in mind when carrying out examinations, assessments and treatment of and for children who are "in need", looked after or about to be looked after and for whom permanence and/or adoption is being considered. The duties are in the:

- Children (Scotland) Act 1995, s.22(2), duty on local authorities in the provision of services to children in need;

- Children (Scotland) Act 1995, s.17(4)(c), duties on local authorities for looked after or about to be looked after children, including when permanence and/or adoption is being considered;

- Adoption and Children (Scotland) Act 2007, s.14, duties on courts and adoption agencies in all decisions about children's adoptions; and

- Adoption and Children (Scotland) Act 2007, s.84(5)(b)(ii), duty on courts when considering applications for permanence orders.

These duties are reinforced in regulations and guidance.

There may at times be uncertainty about the ethnic and cultural background of a child, particularly when the identity or details of the birth father are lacking. However, the use of DNA testing to determine ethnicity is not recommended as these tests have not been adequately evaluated or validated as being accurate for use in this situation. For details, see BAAF and British Society for Human Genetics (BSHG), 2011.

Regardless of whether the child quickly returns to their birth family, remains in care for some time while plans are being made, or has a plan for permanence, the information above is needed to provide current care for the child as well as to complete a high quality health assessment, and to contribute to a comprehensive individual health care plan. This is an opportunity to catch up on missed immunisations, screening and health promotion, to identify previously undiagnosed illnesses and conditions, to assess developmental, social, emotional and mental health needs, and to contribute to a placement that will adequately safeguard the cultural, religious and linguistic background of the child.

Collating health information from various sources including, for instance, the child's GP, community and hospital records, the health visitor, school health service and other specialist services prior to assessment, and organising the transfer of records is a time-consuming activity. Some services have developed an administrative post to ensure access to relevant information and cost-effective use of health professional time.

Engagement

Older children and young people may be reluctant to engage with health practitioners, as they may feel stigmatised by the requirement for statutory health assessments and concerned that sensitive personal information may not be kept confidential. Health professionals must address these barriers to gain the confidence of the young person so that a comprehensive assessment, including health promotion, can be undertaken. This lays the foundation for the young person to begin to accept responsibility for their own health and empowers them to access services.

Who undertakes the initial health assessment?

There is variation across the UK concerning who carries out the initial health assessment. While in many areas, particularly those where the local authority and Trust/health board cover a large geographical area, GPs carry out initial health assessments, in other areas this is largely done by the community paediatrician (or specialist nurse in Scotland and Wales), who is part of a health team for looked after children. Having the initial health assessment completed by their usual GP with whom they are already familiar can provide reassurance to the child at a difficult time, as well as facilitate ready access to the child's own and their family's social and health history, which are key to a comprehensive understanding of the child's health needs. In practice, the child is usually moved to a new GP who will not have ready access to important health information and may lack both the required expertise in the needs of looked after children and the time to carry out a comprehensive statutory initial health assessment.

Many areas offer secondary care for looked after children through development of a specialised and expertly trained health team that includes designated doctors and nurses, medical advisers who are community paediatricians, specialist nurses for looked after children, health visitors, school nurses and midwives. The team may also include GPs with a special interest, who have developed their expertise with looked after children. Some children may be well known to particular services because of an ongoing condition or disability and it may be most appropriate for a health professional from this team to carry out statutory assessments. This skill-based team approach allows the most appropriate professional to engage with individual children and young people with a range of needs, with the added benefit of quality assurance provided by a small team with expertise in the health issues of looked after children, working closely together.

Regardless of the professional designation, it is important that the health professional is trained to a high standard and can demonstrate the competencies appropriate to their role, as outlined in BAAF, 2008, and Royal College of Paediatrics and Child Health and Royal College of Nursing, 2015, which are available in the Health Group section within the members' area of www.corambaaf.org.uk.

Consent Form: consent to obtain and share health information

This form is used to obtain consent to access and share health information relevant to a looked after child and their birth parent. It is **not** used to obtain consent to carry out a health assessment. There is a section to be signed on each IHA and RHA form, indicating consent to carry out the assessment.

Purpose of the form

- To ensure that the birth parent (or other adult with parental responsibility/ies) and child or young person with capacity to consent understand the importance of obtaining comprehensive health information, including family history, for the current and future health and well-being of the child/young person.

- To facilitate access to comprehensive child and family health information at the earliest opportunity, when birth parents are available at the time the child first becomes looked after, in order to avoid problems in obtaining consent at a later date.

- To obtain consent from the birth parent(s) to obtain their health information from various sources.

- To obtain consent to obtain health information about the child or young person from various sources.

- To obtain consent to allow the agency to share health information with health professionals and others involved in provision of health care and planning for the child or young person.

- To obtain consent to allow the agency to share relevant health information with current and future carers.

UNDERTAKING A HEALTH ASSESSMENT

- To allow the child or young person to receive relevant health information at suitable times in the future.
- To accompany Forms M, B, PH, IHA–C, IHA–YP, RHA–C and RHA–YP to access information held by physicians and their records, and permit the sharing of health information as detailed above.

The Consent Form should be signed at the time the child or young person becomes looked after by the local authority, and sent to the agency's health adviser. There are different sections to complete depending on whether the consent relates to information needed about the birth parent or the child/young person, and who will be giving consent, as discussed in Chapter 3. Consent to obtain and share health information may be given by:

- the child/young person;
- the birth parent;
- another adult with parental responsibility/ies;
- an agency.

Who should complete the form?

- **Part A (information about the child/young person)** should be completed by the responsible agency/local authority.
- **Part B (parental consent)** should be completed by the birth parent. Each birth parent should sign a separate form.
- **Part C (child/young person's consent)** should be completed by the child or young person with capacity to consent.
- **Part D** should be completed by the non-parental adult with parental responsibility/ies, or agency representative, **when neither Part B nor C is able to be completed**.

How to use the form

- Complete a separate Consent Form for **each** child in the family.
- A single form may be used for the child or young person and **one** birth parent.
- A copy of the Consent Form must accompany a request for completion of Forms M (mother), B (baby), PH (parental health), IHA–C (initial health assessment for child from birth to nine years), IHA–YP (initial health assessment for young person 10 years and older), RHA–C (review health assessment for child from birth to nine years) and RHA–YP (review health assessment for young person 10 years and older).

To obtain health information relating to a birth parent

- Each birth parent should sign a separate Consent Form for each child becoming looked after.
- The birth parent should sign Part B1.

To obtain health information relating to a child or young person

- A child or young person with capacity to consent should sign Part C. Parental consent is then not needed to access the child's or young person's records.

- For a child or young person without capacity to consent, then either:
  - a birth parent with parental responsibility/ies should sign Part B2; or
  - another adult, or a person representing an agency with parental responsibility/ies, should sign Part D.

Sharing information

Secure email **must** be used when forms containing confidential information are shared with or received from other agencies. Practitioners should be familiar with the systems in use in their locality and protocols for sharing confidential information.

Part A and procedure for the agency and social worker

- When the child or young person becomes looked after, the agency must ensure, so far as possible, that the Consent Form is completed by the appropriate individual/s, considering the principles outlined in the section on consent.

- Agencies must ensure that social workers are adequately trained to undertake this task, with a clear understanding of what health information is needed, why it is important, and how it will be used. They must have the ability to communicate this information effectively and answer any questions that arise. Agency policies and procedures must make it clear that each case requires proper assessment and the exercise of judgement concerning the child's or young person's understanding and capacity to consent.

Important parent and child health information

It is important to document a variety of health information that can have implications for the child's short- and long-term health and development. We have given examples below of parent and child information and why this is important. Further information on child health issues and development is available in Merredew and Sampeys, 2015.

Mother

- Maternal use of alcohol during the pregnancy – exposure to alcohol can produce a typical facial pattern, growth retardation and permanent neurocognitive deficits that may be mild or profound in degree. A known history of alcohol use in pregnancy is invaluable in making the diagnosis of foetal alcohol spectrum disorder (FASD).

- Maternal use of drugs during the pregnancy – neonatal abstinence syndrome or "withdrawal" occurs when the foetus has become addicted to substances used by the mother. Drugs such as heroin and cocaine can cause various types of cognitive deficit.

- Intravenous drug injection is a significant risk factor for transmission of hepatitis and HIV during pregnancy and delivery – it is important to know whether the mother has these infections so that her child can receive early screening.

Father and mother

- Learning disability and mental health issues such as schizophrenia and depression may have a genetic element – it is important to obtain details and may be necessary to contact consultants to confirm a diagnosis. As the child develops, this information contributes to an assessment.
- Although the presence in the family of a genetic condition such as Huntington's disease may not have any impact during childhood, this information will become important in adulthood when genetic counselling should be offered and screening considered.

Child

- Immunisation history – the child should receive any missed immunisations.
- Birth history – birth trauma, prematurity, birth weight and condition affect growth and development.
- Neonatal history – withdrawal symptoms can indicate antenatal substance exposure and may have long-term implications.
- Early development – milestones indicate developmental progress and need for intervention.
- Past and ongoing health issues – health professionals and carers should be aware of illnesses, injuries, operations and current health issues as they may impact on future health.
- Neglect and abuse – these may have a profound effect on physical and emotional health and development.
- Mental and emotional health – although some children will present with difficulties in these areas, in other cases recording information about the child's early emotional, social and behavioural development will contribute to an overall understanding of emerging or potential future difficulties and need for intervention.

- The agency social worker has a crucial role in taking forward completion of the Consent Form in advance of the health assessment. It is important that the necessary consents are available in good time for the health professional to access the child's and parents' health information before he or she carries out the assessment.
- The birth parent gives consent to access and share their own health information by signing Part B1.
- Consent to access and share the child's health information is given by the birth parent (signing Part B2) or other adult (signing Part D) or by the child (signing Part C). Taking into account the age and development of the child or young person, the legal

situation and who holds parental responsibility/ies, the social worker will need to consider who should give consent.

- A child or young person is not able to consent unless they have the capacity. This is a decision for the health professional (not the social work practitioner or agency) – does the child or young person understand the nature and consequences of consenting? In England and Wales, the principles of the Fraser Guidelines apply. In Scotland, the relevant provision is s.2(4) of the Age of Legal Capacity (Scotland) Act 1991.

- Although parental consent is not required if the child or young person has the capacity to consent, it is best practice in most circumstances to involve the birth parent(s) in the process and seek their agreement as well.

- Part A contains important demographic information, including contact details, for the GPs of the child and parents, that will allow the assessing health professional to contact them for necessary health information. It must be completed in full by the social worker.

- The social worker must state the name and contact details of the agency health adviser to whom the form should be returned.

Part B and procedure for the social worker and birth parent

- Since it is important for the child's current and future health and well-being to have comprehensive health information about both birth parents and their respective families, every effort should be made to contact both birth parents, so that each can complete a Consent Form (signing Part B1).

- Informed consent rests on the individual having the capacity to understand the implications of consenting. The social worker should explain to the birth parent that comprehensive health history is needed concerning the child, and that relevant health information, including family health problems, is needed concerning the birth parent. The social worker should also explain that relevant health information will need to be shared, and with whom.

- Part B should be completed by the birth parent, who may give consent, for two different purposes:

    1. To access comprehensive health information about the birth parent and his or her family, and share this as relevant to the child's situation. Consent for this can only be given by the birth parent.

    2. To access comprehensive health information about the child or young person, and share information as appropriate. However, this consent is only needed if the child or young person does not have the capacity to consent on his or her own behalf.

- When signing Part B at the time that the child or young person becomes looked after, the birth parent with parental responsibility/ies for a child or young person who does not have capacity to consent gives consent for ongoing and continuous assessment and planning for the child, unless the consent is specifically withdrawn at a future date. While this is useful in situations where the agency is unable to maintain contact with a birth parent, it would be considered best practice to involve the birth parent(s) in ongoing health assessment and planning.

UNDERTAKING A HEALTH ASSESSMENT

- It is also important to remember that a child or young person who did not have capacity to consent when he or she became looked after may gain capacity whilst in the care system. In that situation, his or her consent for accessing and sharing information should be sought, using Part C.
- Part B of a single Consent Form may be used to obtain consent from one birth parent to access and share their own health information and the child's information if he or she does not have capacity to consent. The other birth parent must sign Part B1 of a second Consent Form to allow access to his or her health information.
- If more than one child becomes looked after at the same time, a separate Consent Form should be completed by *each* parent for *each* child, so that information can be accessed and shared on behalf of each child.
- The social worker should witness the signatures.

Part C and procedure for the social worker and child or young person with capacity to consent

- When the child or young person has capacity to consent, then the social worker will need to explain the same issues as outlined in Part B to the child or young person, using language that they can understand.
- The social worker or other appropriate professional should witness the signature.

Part D and procedure for the social worker and an adult with parental responsibility/ies, or a representative authorised to give consent on behalf of an agency with parental responsibility/ies, under a court order

- The agency should be aware of situations where the child has a legal guardian who may sign this consent at Part D1.
- When the agency has parental responsibility/ies under a court order, Part D should be signed at Part D2 by a senior representative of the agency with sufficient authority to sign on behalf of the local authority.
- The name and professional designation of the person giving consent must be recorded.
- The social worker or other appropriate professional should witness the signature.

The completed Consent Form

- The signed Consent Form should be sent to the agency's health adviser. A copy should be attached to Forms M, B, PH, IHA–C, IHA–YP, RHA–C and RHA–YP (as appropriate).

Form M: mother's health

Purpose of the form

- To provide information on the health and behaviour of the mother in pregnancy, during delivery and postnatally, which may have implications for her child's health, development or behaviour immediately or in the future.

- To facilitate the sharing of relevant health information with the child's new GP and carers to enable them to provide appropriate care for the child.

- To provide information for the child that may help them, in the future, to form an understanding of their origins and identity.

Who should complete the form?

- **Part A** should be completed by the agency/local authority.
- **Part B** should be completed by a doctor or a midwife (from the mother's records).

Why this information is important

Form M should be completed for all children and young people becoming looked after, preferably shortly after they come into care in order to prevent valuable information being lost to them and their carers. Pregnancy and neonatal history remain essential information for older children and young people as this period of life forms the foundation on which future health, development and, to some extent, behaviour rests. The information on Form M is essential to the completion of a comprehensive initial health assessment and development of the health care plan. Details of high-risk behaviour in this or a previous pregnancy are extremely helpful, e.g. use of alcohol or drugs, including IV injection. It also enables a carer, or the child or young person when they reach adulthood, to provide a health professional with information about the child's earliest history that may be essential to the making of an accurate diagnosis.

For an older child, obtaining the mother's consent and tracing her records can be problematic but the information is invaluable to adopted people and those individuals who are, or have been, in long-term care, both in terms of their health and in the formation of their identity.

Consent

The mother's consent to her information being shared with the agency should be obtained on the CoramBAAF Consent Form. A copy of the signed Consent Form **must** accompany a request for the completion of Form M. Mothers are most likely to sign the consent form if a professional/social worker whom they know/trust explains how important the information on the form is for the future health and well-being of their child. Mothers should be reassured that such information will only be used as necessary and will remain confidential to the agency and the child's doctors and carer, although they should know that the child may be given information if it is necessary for their health and well-being.

UNDERTAKING A HEALTH ASSESSMENT

In Scotland, the Adoption (Disclosure of Information and Medical Information about Natural Parents) (Scotland) Regulations 2009, SSI 2009/268, may be helpful in obtaining certain medical information about the child's family, if adoption is the plan for the child. Regulation 11 states that where the agency has not been able to obtain information about whether there is 'any history of genetically transmissible or other significant disease' in the birth mother's or father's families, a medical practitioner, such as a birth parent's GP, must disclose such information to the adoption agency on request.

Sharing information

Secure email **must** be used when sharing relevant information on these forms with other agencies. Practitioners should be familiar with the systems in use in their locality and protocols for sharing confidential information.

Part A and procedure for the agency/local authority

- Part A contains the information required to identify the mother of a looked after child, and should be completed in full by the agency.
- In order to maintain confidentiality, it is essential to indicate correctly the name and contact details of the agency health adviser to whom the form should be returned.
- A commissioning letter signed by the agency medical adviser should be sent to the hospital where the child was born. A copy of the signed Consent Form **must** accompany this request for the completion of Form M.

Part B and procedure for the doctor or midwife

- Part B should be completed by a doctor or midwife (from the mother's records), providing full details wherever possible. Whoever signs it will be responsible for the accuracy of the information.
- Guidance for the health professional completing the form is provided on the form itself.
- The completed form should be returned to the agency health adviser indicated in Part A.

See Case Study 1 in Chapter 7 for an example of completion of Form M.

Form B: baby's health

Purpose of the form

- To provide information on the child's health and behaviour in the neonatal period, relevant to their current and future health care, and to inform decisions regarding future placements.
- To contribute to the written information given by the agency to prospective adopters or foster carers, to enable them to care appropriately for the child.

The initial health assessment

- To provide information for the new GP, in accordance with regulations throughout the UK.

- To provide essential information for the child about their earliest days, the availability of which will be greatly valued by the child when he or she reaches adulthood, and which will promote their sense of self and identity.

Who should complete the form?

- **Part A** should be completed by the agency/local authority.

- **Part B** should be completed by a doctor, midwife or senior nurse (from the birth records of the child).

Why this information is important

Form B should be completed for all children and young people becoming looked after, preferably shortly after they come into care in order to prevent valuable information being lost to them and their carers. Pregnancy and neonatal history remain essential information for older children and young people as this period of life forms the foundation on which future health, development and, to some extent, behaviour rests. The information on Form B is essential to the completion of a comprehensive health assessment and health care plan. It also enables a carer, or the child or young person when they reach adulthood, to provide a health professional with information about the child's earliest history that may be essential to the making of an accurate diagnosis.

Tracing the early records of an older child can be problematic but the information is invaluable to adopted people and those individuals who are, or have been, in long-term care, both in terms of their health and in the formation of their identity. Community health records are often invaluable sources of relevant information.

Consent

Consent is required to access the information requested on Form B; the CoramBAAF Consent Form is a convenient way of recording this. It **must** accompany a request to complete Form B and provides guidance as to who may give consent to access health information.

Sharing information

Secure email **must** be used when sharing relevant information on these forms with other agencies. Practitioners should be familiar with the systems in use in their locality and protocols for sharing confidential information.

Part A and procedure for the agency/local authority

- Part A contains the information that identifies the looked after child and their mother, and should be completed in full by the agency.

- In order to maintain confidentiality, it is essential to correctly indicate the name and contact details of the agency health adviser to whom the form should be returned.

- A commissioning letter signed by the agency medical adviser should be sent to the hospital where the child was born. A copy of the signed Consent Form **must** accompany a request for the completion of Form B.

Part B and procedure for the doctor, midwife or senior nurse

- Part B should be completed by a doctor, midwife or senior nurse from the birth records of the child; it is essential to provide full details. Whoever signs it will be responsible for the accuracy of the information on it.

- Guidance for the health professional completing the form is provided on the form itself.

- This form will cover the essential information needed for most children. However, if the child has had a very complicated neonatal course, then further reports or a discharge summary from the hospital records should be attached.

- The completed form should be returned to the agency health adviser indicated in Part A.

See Case Study 1 in Chapter 7 for an example of completion of Form B.

Form PH: report on health of birth parent

Purpose of the form

- To provide information that will contribute to the care of the child's health, both currently and in the future.

- To provide a family health history that will assist in planning for the child's placement.

- To provide an opportunity to discuss with birth parents the health history of their extended families that, in view of increasing genetic knowledge, could prove to be of importance throughout their child's life and possibly for their children as well.

- To demonstrate to the child later on that their birth parents gave thought and consideration to their child's future welfare.

Who should complete the form?

- **Part A** should be completed by the agency/local authority.
- **Part B** should be completed by the birth parent together with the social worker. Each birth parent should complete a separate form.

Why this information is important

Form PH should be completed for all children and young people becoming looked after, preferably shortly after they come into care, to prevent valuable information being lost to them and their carers. The information on Form PH is essential to the completion of a comprehensive initial health assessment (IHA) and health care plan; however, attendance

The initial health assessment

of the birth parent(s) at the IHA is still highly valued. It also enables a carer, or the child or young person when they reach adulthood, to provide a health professional with information about the child's family history that may be essential to the making of an accurate diagnosis.

In some cases, the agency medical adviser may wish to obtain further information from the parent's GP or specialist, provided that informed consent has been given (for example, on the CoramBAAF Consent Form). The IHA provides an opportunity to obtain additional information from birth parents, and they should be encouraged to attend.

In Scotland, the Adoption (Disclosure of Information and Medical Information about Natural Parents) (Scotland) Regulations 2009, SSI 2009/268, may be helpful in obtaining certain medical information about the child's family, if adoption is the plan for the child. Regulation 11 states that where the agency has not been able to obtain information about whether there is 'any history of genetically transmissible or other significant disease' in the birth mother's or father's families, a medical practitioner, such as a birth parent's GP, must disclose such information to the adoption agency on request.

Sharing information

Secure email **must** be used when sharing relevant information on these forms with other agencies. Practitioners should be familiar with the systems in use in their locality and protocols for sharing confidential information.

Procedure for the social worker and birth parent

- Part A contains important demographic information and should be completed in full by the agency social worker. It is essential to indicate correctly the name and contact details of the agency health adviser to whom the form should be returned.

- The social worker must ensure that birth parents understand the purpose of the form and appreciate that the information they give about their own and their families' health history is of great value to the current and future welfare of their child. This should be made clear to them before they are asked to sign the Consent Form, which may be needed to access additional information from their GP or consultant and subsequently to share relevant information with others involved in the care of their child.

- The social worker should indicate whether or not a birth parent has a learning difficulty. This information is essential for the child, and may affect the birth parent's ability to understand and complete the form. If a birth parent is unable to read or write, the social worker should complete the form in their presence. People who speak English fluently may have difficulty in writing it and may need help.

- Where there are difficulties in obtaining information from a birth father, the social worker may be able to obtain information from other sources, such as the other birth parent or a family member, e.g. grandparent. Although even limited information is of value to a child, the form should make clear that the information recorded is second-hand; the name of the source and their relationship to the birth parent should be included on the form.

UNDERTAKING A HEALTH ASSESSMENT

- On completion, the form should be passed to the agency medical adviser and given to the health professional examining the child, to assist with completion of the health assessment.
- Occasionally another professional, for example, a lawyer, may assist the birth parent with completion of this form.

See Case Studies 1, 2 and 3 in Chapter 7 for examples of completion of Form PH.

Form IHA–C: initial health assessment for child from birth to nine years

Purpose of the form

- To help health practitioners fulfil the regulatory requirements that exist throughout the UK for each looked after child to have a holistic, comprehensive health assessment and a health care plan in place prior to the first looked after children review.
- To provide the framework for this initial health assessment and provision of a written summary health report that will be used to formulate the health recommendations for the child care plan.
- To record the child's wishes and feelings regarding their present and future health, and provide an opportunity to discuss any concerns.
- To provide carers and professionals with important health information on the child, and provide a foundation for future health reviews.
- To provide the basis for reports for adoption panels, discussions with prospective adopters at matching and possibly to inform court proceedings.
- To provide the child with details of their past health history on reaching adulthood and lay the foundations for the involvement of children in their own health care.

Who should complete the form?

- **Part A** should be completed by the agency/social worker.
- **Part B** should be completed by the examining health professional, either a doctor or a nurse.
- **Part C** should be completed by the examining health professional.
- **Part D** may be used for data collection if desired by the responsible looked after children health team.

Quality assurance

The forms have been revised in accordance with feedback collected over 10 years and have undergone wide consultation. They are designed for use throughout the UK,

The initial health assessment

although it is recognised that regulations across the four countries differ and that practice varies across regions depending on local circumstances. To ensure that the forms meet local needs and processes, they may be used flexibly – for example, if information has been recorded previously and is accessible within the health record, it is not necessary to duplicate it. Similarly, not every question or prompt will need to be followed for each child, and clinical judgement should be exercised.

Part B should be completed by the assessing health professional, who must have relevant experience and training to at least Level 3 of the RCPCH and RCN Intercollegiate Competencies. Regulations in England and Northern Ireland require a doctor to undertake the assessment; however, in Scotland and Wales, this may be carried out by a doctor or nurse. If the child is followed in a specialist or disability clinic, it may be most appropriate for a practitioner from that team to complete the assessment.

This examination and assessment are not required if they have already been carried out by a suitably qualified health professional in the three months immediately preceding the date on which the child began to be looked after by the local authority. However, the existing health plan should be reviewed and updated to take account of the child's changed circumstances. Additionally, there may well be circumstances in which the child's history or current presentation warrants further comprehensive examination or assessment. This will be a matter for individual clinical judgement.

Sharing information

Secure email **must** be used when sharing relevant information on these forms with other agencies. Practitioners should be familiar with the systems in use in their locality and protocols for sharing confidential information.

Part A and procedure for the social worker prior to health assessment

- Part A contains important demographic, social and legal information that is required by the assessing health professional prior to the assessment and **must be completed in full by the social worker/local authority**.

- The social worker must state the name and contact details of the agency health adviser to whom the form should be returned. The child's legal status and holder/s of parental responsibility/ies must be indicated.

Consent to access health information

- In order to meet standards set out in national guidance, information on past health history, including birth and family history, is required for completion of the health assessment and summary report, and should ideally be collated prior to the health appointment; CoramBAAF Forms M (mother), B (baby) and PH (parental health) can be used to collect this information. In addition, information held in the GP records together with other available medical and health reports, particularly where the child has a disability or serious medical condition, should be obtained.

- **In Scotland**, the Adoption (Disclosure of Information and Medical Information about Natural Parents) (Scotland) Regulations 2009, SSI 2009/268, may be helpful in obtaining certain medical information about the child's family, if adoption is the plan

UNDERTAKING A HEALTH ASSESSMENT

for the child. Regulation 11 says that where the agency has not been able to obtain information about whether there is 'any history of genetically transmissible or other significant disease' in the birth mother's or father's families, a medical practitioner, such as a birth parent's GP, must disclose such information to the adoption agency on request.

- A signed CoramBAAF Consent Form should accompany the request to complete Forms M, B, PH, IHA–C and IHA–YP to facilitate access to additional child or family health information.

Consent for health assessment

- The social worker should make every effort to obtain informed consent for the health assessment in advance, by having the consent section at the end of Part A of this form signed. This consent, unless the child has capacity to give his or her own consent, should be obtained from:

  - a birth parent with parental responsibility/ies; or
  - another adult with parental responsibility/ies; or
  - an authorised representative of any agency holding parental responsibility/ies.

- The child with capacity to consent may do so by signing the consent section at the start of Part B of this form at the time of the health assessment.

- Consent from birth parent(s) is best obtained at the time of placement. The birth parent(s) may give consent by signing the looked after children documents, and these should be available for the assessing health professional on request. Alternatively, the birth parent(s) may give consent by signing the consent section at the end of Part A of this form.

- The child's social worker should provide the assessing health professional with background details and the reason for the child being looked after, for example, a child protection or core assessment report. It is the social worker's responsibility to prepare the child, parents and carer for the assessment. If the child's *Personal Child Health Record* (red book) is not already in the possession of the carer, the social worker should obtain it from the parents and ensure that it is brought to the health assessment.

- It is good practice for the social worker, and birth parent(s) where appropriate, to attend the assessment as well as the carer, thus ensuring that the health professional has up-to-date information on the child's background and family and personal history, and is able to receive directly any comments regarding the child's health. **The social worker should advise the health professional if there are any concerns about personal safety for all those attending.** The social worker should also alert the health professional to any addresses on the form that must not be shared with other family members.

- The social worker should ensure that arrangements are made for an interpreter or signer to be present if necessary.

- **The agency/social worker should be aware that it is the expectation of the looked after children health team that they should be notified when actions from the recommendations in Part C are carried out.**

The initial health assessment

Part B and procedure for the assessing health professional

- Part B should be completed by the assessing health professional, who must have relevant experience and training to at least Level 3 of the RCPCH and RCN Intercollegiate Competencies. Regulations in England and Northern Ireland require a doctor to undertake the assessment; however, in Scotland and Wales this may be carried out by a doctor or nurse.

- Services should have a mechanism for identifying which health professional is best placed to undertake the assessment. If the child is already known to the community child health team, a paediatrician who knows the child may be better placed to provide a comprehensive report. If the IHA is to be carried out by a health professional who is not part of the looked after children health team, a commissioning letter signed by the agency medical adviser should accompany the request.

- It is important for any assessing health professional to seek advice and guidance when needed from a senior colleague with expertise. Although some specialist nurses have expertise in physical examination, medical oversight should be in place, and there should be an agreed pathway for the child whose IHA is completed by a nurse to see a doctor if needed.

- The purpose of the assessment should first be explained to the child, parent(s) and carer.

- The child with capacity to consent to the health assessment should indicate his or her consent by signing the consent at the start of Part B.

- Those present at the assessment should be listed at the beginning of Part B.

- It may be appropriate to see the child and the carer on their own for part of the assessment. It would also be appropriate to see the birth parent(s) alone to obtain their health history.

- The form should record the child's wishes and feelings regarding their present and future health and well-being.

- The forms are intended as guidance and should not replace clinical judgement. A box can be left blank if the question or issue is not relevant and should be marked N/A for "not applicable" to indicate that the practitioner has considered it.

- The extent of the physical examination will depend on the age of the child and its appropriateness within the clinical context. For example, examination of the genitalia would not be routine in an older child if there is no clinical indication. Practitioners should clearly document what physical examination has been carried out.

- With appropriate consent (for example, using the CoramBAAF Consent Form), health professionals should use all available information, such as community health, GP and hospital records, to inform the assessment. Additional information that is thought to be relevant may be available from other sources within the child's care network. The source of all information should be documented.

UNDERTAKING A HEALTH ASSESSMENT

> ### Health information relevant to the IHA
>
> Forms PH, M and B should be completed for all looked after children, and additional health information relevant to the IHA may be obtained from:
>
> - community health records, including speech and language, physiotherapy and occupational therapy;
> - health visitor records;
> - school nursing service;
> - GP records;
> - hospital records;
> - CAMHS and clinical psychology;
> - expert reports and parenting psychology reports from the local authority;
> - parental health records provided by the local authority legal department from care proceedings;
> - CoramBAAF Carers' reports.

- For refugee and trafficked children, the impact on their health of their country of origin and route taken; experiences en route; entry point into the UK; infectious diseases; the impact of displacement, separation and loss; physical, emotional and sexual trauma; sexual health; and mental health should be considered. See Additional Resources for websites providing information on worldwide prevalence rates of HIV/AIDS and hepatitis as well as country-specific immunisation schedules and uptake.

- Since Part B may contain personal and sensitive information about other family members, as well as the child, it should be retained in the child's health record and treated with the utmost care with respect to confidentiality. For adoption only, a copy of the entire form must be sent to the child's adoption agency.

- Practitioners should be sensitive to the language used as this report may be shared across agencies, released in court proceedings and accessed by the child in the future.

- To the extent that is appropriate to their age and development, the issues raised in the report should be discussed with the child and they should be aware of what will happen next, including the sharing of information.

- For children placed out of area, the entire completed form, including Part B, should be sent to the looked after children health team in the responsible/placing area.

Part C: Summary health report

- Part C is the summary report and health recommendations for the care plan. All of Part C will be needed by the social worker who has responsibility to formulate the health care plan, and the Independent Reviewing Officer (IRO)/reviewing officer who has responsibility to review the child's care plan. Completion of Part C in its entirety will provide the information required to fulfil the statutory requirements of the health care plan.

- Part C should include an analysis of the child's personal and family health history and the implications these have for the child's current and future health and care needs. Part C will be shared with adoption and fostering agencies.

- Part C should usually be completed by the assessing health professional. Occasionally it may be necessary for the looked after children health team from the responsible/placing authority to assist in completion of Part C to ensure a comprehensive report.

- Health recommendations for the child care plan should be specific, time-bound and clearly identify the person responsible for each action. The plan should include upcoming appointments with dates and any outstanding issues such as immunisations. **It is the expectation of the looked after children health team that they should be notified when actions are carried out.**

- Part C should include a list of all those who receive a copy of Part C; the list should include all those with responsibility for implementing recommendations for the child care plan.

- Part C can be used as the basis for discussion with current and future carers, provided informed consent has been obtained to disclose the information. **In Scotland**, regulations state that prospective adopters must be given full information about a child at the time of placement, including medical information on the child and his or her birth family. **In England, Wales and Northern Ireland**, it is good practice to disclose all relevant health information to prospective adopters.

- Part C may be released in court proceedings and may be accessed by the child at a later date, so it is important to be sensitive to confidentiality and the use of language.

- Statutory guidance for England states that the lead health record for a looked after child should be the GP-held record and that the entire initial health assessment and health plan, and subsequent review assessments and plans, should be part of that record.

- Consent issues when sharing third party information need to be carefully considered in light of what is relevant to the child and in their best interests.

Part D: Data collection and audit

- This is an optional section that looked after children health teams may customise for their local data collection.

- In England, the National Tariff checklist, developed as a quality assurance tool for health assessments of children placed out of area, may be inserted here.

See Case Studies 1 and 3 in Chapter 7 for examples of completion of selected sections of Form IHA–C.

UNDERTAKING A HEALTH ASSESSMENT

Form IHA–YP: initial health assessment for young person 10 years and older

Purpose of the form

- To create an opportunity for discussion with the young person about their health concerns, including physical and mental development, relationships, sexual health, possible use of tobacco, drugs and alcohol, and to encourage them to begin to assume responsibility for their own health.

- The same purposes as those of Form IHA–C.

Who should complete the form?

- **Part A** should be completed by the agency/social worker.

- **Part B** should be completed by the examining health professional, either a doctor or a nurse.

- **Part C** should be completed by the examining health professional.

- **Part D** may be used for data collection if desired by the responsible looked after children health team.

Guidance

All of the comments and guidance under Form IHA–C are equally applicable to Form IHA–YP, with the following specific comments.

Part A and procedure for the social worker prior to health assessment: consent for health assessment

- The social worker should make every effort to obtain informed consent for the health assessment in advance. This consent should be sought from:

  - the young person, if he or she has capacity to consent; or

  - a birth parent with parental responsibility/ies; or

  - another adult with parental responsibility/ies; or

  - an authorised representative of any agency holding parental responsibility/ies.

- With increasing maturity and understanding, it is to be expected that many, or perhaps most, young people will have capacity to consent to health assessment, and will take an increasingly active part in their own health care. If the social worker has any concerns about the young person's capacity to consent, they should seek advice from the health professional.

The initial health assessment

Part B and procedure for the assessing health professional

- There is a section for the young person to sign, giving their informed consent to the assessment. With increasing maturity and understanding, it is to be expected that many, or perhaps most, young people will have capacity to consent to health assessment, and will take an increasingly active part in their own health care.

- The emphasis should be on engaging the young person in the assessment of their own health and encouraging responsible health behaviour and a healthy lifestyle, including discussing their hopes and aspirations, rather than on completing yet another form.

- Those present at the assessment should be listed at the beginning of Part B. It is important to note that young people may not discuss sensitive and personal information unless confidentiality can be assured. At the outset, the issue of confidentiality should be raised with the young person and the limits of confidentiality explained. Carers or other adults should not be present during assessment unless the young person specifically gives permission. It may, however, be helpful to speak to the carer(s) alone. It would also be appropriate to see the birth parent(s) alone to obtain their health history.

- The issues raised in the report must be discussed with the young person and great care must be taken to respect confidentiality. Explicit consent for the release of personal and sensitive information to others in the health care team, to carers, to the school, etc, must be negotiated.

See Case Study 2 in Chapter 7 for an example of completion of selected sections of Form IHA–YP.

5 The review health assessment

The frequency of review health assessments for looked after children is specified in regulations or guidance for each UK country but may be carried out more frequently if there is a particular concern about a child. See Chapter 2 on legal issues for details.

The request for a review health assessment is usually initiated by the child's social worker. It is often nurse-led, and provides an opportunity to follow up on earlier issues raised and recommendations made in the previous Health Care Plans (HCP). It is also an opportunity to monitor access to specialised services, as well as to offer health promotion appropriate to the child's age and stage of development. Each health assessment is a further chance for the young person to develop knowledge, skills and attitudes to assist them in becoming responsible for their own health.

Form RHA–C: review health assessment for child from birth to nine years

Purpose of the form

- To help health practitioners fulfil the regulatory requirements throughout the UK for each looked after child to have a periodic health review and modification of their health care plan.

- To provide a holistic review of the health and development of looked after children, to determine if previous health care plans have been carried out, to identify new issues and to provide a written summary health report that will be used to formulate the health recommendations for the child care plan.

- To offer carers and children (to the extent that is age and developmentally appropriate) an opportunity to discuss any particular concerns about their health care with a health professional.

- To provide an ongoing opportunity to engage children in their own health care.

- To focus on health promotion appropriate to the age and development of the child.

The review health assessment

Who should complete the form?

- **Part A** should be completed by the agency/social worker.
- **Part B** should be completed by the examining health professional, either a doctor or nurse.
- **Part C** should be completed by the examining health professional.
- **Part D** may be used for data collection if desired by the responsible looked after children health team.

Quality assurance

The forms have been revised in accordance with feedback collected over 10 years and have undergone wide consultation. They are designed for use throughout the UK, although it is recognised that regulations across the four countries differ and that practice varies across regions depending on local circumstances. To ensure that the forms meet local needs and processes, they may be used flexibly – for example, if information has been recorded previously and is accessible within the health record, it is not necessary to duplicate it. Similarly, not every question or prompt will need to be followed for each child, and clinical judgement can be exercised.

Part B should be completed by the assessing health professional, who must have relevant experience and training to at least Level 3 of the RCPCH and RCN Intercollegiate Competencies. If the child is followed in a specialist or disability clinic, it may be most appropriate for a practitioner from that team to complete the assessment.

Sharing information

Secure email **must** be used when sharing any of the information on these forms with other agencies. Practitioners should be familiar with the systems in use in their locality and protocols for sharing confidential information.

Part A and procedure for the social worker prior to health assessment

- Part A contains important demographic, social and legal information that is required by the assessing health professional prior to the assessment and **must be completed in full by the social worker/local authority.**
- The social worker must state the name and contact details of the agency health adviser to whom the form should be returned. The child's legal status and holder/s of parental responsibility/ies must be indicated.

Consent for health assessment

- The social worker should make every effort to obtain informed consent for the health assessment in advance, by having the consent section at the end of Part A of this form signed. This consent, unless the child has capacity to give his or her own consent, should be obtained from:
    - a birth parent with parental responsibility/ies; or

UNDAKING A HEALTH ASSESSMENT

- another adult with parental responsibility/ies; or
- an authorised representative of any agency holding parental responsibility/ies.

- The child with capacity to consent may do so by signing the consent section at the start of Part B of this form at the time of the health assessment.

- Although it is best practice to obtain consent at the time of each health assessment, this may not always be possible. When consent has been obtained at the time of placement, a copy should be available for the assessing health professional on request. It must be remembered that a child may have developed capacity to consent since earlier consent was given by a parent or other adult.

- When a child is in a concurrent, Foster to Adopt or long-term fostering placement, a prospective adoptive parent or foster carer may have delegated authority to consent to health assessments. The social worker should provide a copy of the record of the delegated responsibility arrangement for the child's health file, and document this in the section on consent.

- **In England or Wales**, when a child has a placement order and is placed with prospective adopter(s), the prospective adopter(s) will have shared parental responsibility/ies and may give consent for health assessment, assuming that the child does not have capacity to consent.

- **In Northern Ireland**, prospective adopters do not have parental responsibility for a child placed with them, although on occasion they may have delegated authority to consent for health assessment, assuming that the child does not have capacity to consent.

- **In Scotland**, when a child is subject to a permanence order, the carers may have the parental responsibility to consent to medical treatment or delegated authority to do so, assuming that the child does not have capacity to consent.

- **Consent to access health information**: In most instances, complete health information on the child and family will have been obtained at the initial health assessment. Occasionally there may be instances when a copy of the CoramBAAF Consent Form must accompany a request for additional health information or records, for example, when CoramBAAF Forms M (mother), B (baby) or PH (parental health) were not completed for the initial health assessment (IHA).

- The child's social worker should provide the assessing health professional with details regarding any change to social, family or educational circumstances. It is the social worker's responsibility to prepare the child, parents and carer for the assessment.

- The child's social worker should provide the assessing health professional with a copy of the most recent health care plan and an updated report including any actions or outcomes from the last assessment. If the child's *Personal Child Health Record* (red book) is not already in the possession of the carer, the social worker should obtain it from the parents and ensure that it is brought to the health assessment.

- It is good practice for the social worker, and birth parent(s) where appropriate, to attend the assessment as well as the carer, thus ensuring that the health professional has up-to-date information on the child's background and family and personal history, and is able to receive directly any comments regarding the child's health. **The social worker should advise the health professional if there are any concerns about**

The review health assessment

personal safety for all those attending. The social worker should also alert the health professional to any addresses on the form that must not be shared with other family members.

- The social worker should ensure that arrangements are made for an interpreter or signer to be present if necessary.

- **The agency/social worker should be aware that it is the expectation of the looked after children health team that they should be notified when actions from the recommendations in Part C are carried out.**

Part B and procedure for the assessing health professional

- Part B should be completed by the assessing health professional, who must have relevant experience and training to at least Level 3 of the RCPCH and RCN Intercollegiate Competencies.

- Services should have a mechanism for identifying which health professional is best placed to undertake the assessment. If the child is already known to the community child health team, a practitioner who knows the child may be better placed to provide a comprehensive report. If the assessment is to be carried out by a health professional who is not part of the looked after children health team, a commissioning letter signed by the agency medical adviser should accompany the request.

- It is important for any assessing health professional to seek advice and guidance, when needed, from a senior colleague with expertise. Although some specialist nurses have expertise in physical examination, medical oversight should be in place, and there should be an agreed pathway for the child, whose assessment was completed by a nurse, to see a doctor if needed.

- To provide continuity of care, the assessing health practitioner should always have a copy of the previous health assessment/s, including the entire IHA and most recent RHA form, a copy of the most recent health care plan, an updated report from the social worker including any actions or outcomes from the last assessment, relevant reports from other health professionals, and a copy of the *Personal Child Health Record* or *Carer-Held Health Record*.

- The purpose of the assessment should first be explained to the child, parent(s) and carer.

- As indicated in Part A, the child with capacity to consent to the health assessment should indicate his or her consent by signing the consent at the start of Part B.

- Those present at the assessment should be listed at the start of Part B.

- It may be appropriate to see the child and the carer on their own for part of the assessment.

- The form should record the child's wishes and feelings regarding their present and future health and well-being.

- The forms are intended as guidance and should not replace clinical judgement. A box can be left blank if the question or issue is not relevant, and should be marked N/A for "not applicable" to indicate that the practitioner has considered it.

UNDERTAKING A HEALTH ASSESSMENT

- The extent of the physical examination will depend on the age of the child and its appropriateness within the clinical context. For example, examination of the genitalia would not be routine in an older child if there is no clinical indication. Practitioners should clearly document what physical examination has been carried out.

- With appropriate consent (for example, using the CoramBAAF Consent Form), health professionals should use all available information, such as community health, GP and hospital records, to inform the assessment. Additional information that is thought to be relevant may be available from other sources within the child's care network. The source of all information should be documented.

- For refugee and trafficked children, any ongoing impact on their health of their country of origin and route taken, experiences en route, infectious diseases, the impact of displacement, separation and loss, physical, emotional and sexual trauma, and mental health should be considered. See Additional Resources for websites providing information on worldwide prevalence rates of HIV/AIDS and hepatitis, as well as country-specific immunisation schedules and uptake.

- Since Part B may contain personal and sensitive information about other family members as well as the child, it should be retained in the child's health record, and treated with the utmost care with respect to confidentiality. For adoption only, a copy of the entire form will be sent to the child's adoption agency.

- Practitioners should be sensitive to the language used as this report may be shared across agencies, released in court proceedings and accessed by the child in the future.

- To the extent that is appropriate to their age and development, the issues raised in the report should be discussed with the child and they should be aware of what will happen next, including the sharing of information.

- For children placed out of area, the entire completed form, including Part B, should be sent to the looked after children health team in the responsible/placing area.

Part C: Summary health report

- Part C is the summary report and health recommendations for the care plan. All of Part C will be needed by the social worker who has responsibility to formulate the health care plan, and the Independent Reviewing Officer/reviewing officer who has responsibility to review the child's care plan. Completion of Part C in its entirety will provide the information required to fulfil the statutory requirements for the health care plan.

- Part C should include an analysis of the child's personal and family health history and the implications these have for the child's current and future health and care needs. Part C will be shared with adoption and fostering agencies.

- Part C should usually be completed by the assessing health professional. Occasionally, it may be necessary for the looked after children's health team from the responsible/placing authority to assist in the completion of Part C to ensure a comprehensive report.

- Health recommendations for the care plan should be specific, time-bound and clearly identify the person responsible for each action. The plan should include upcoming

The review health assessment

appointments with dates and any outstanding issues such as immunisations. **It is the expectation of the looked after children health team that they should be notified when actions are carried out.**

- Part C should include a list of all those who receive a copy of it; the list should include all those with responsibility for implementing recommendations for the child care plan.

- Part C can be used as the basis for discussion with current and future carers, provided informed consent has been obtained to disclose the information. **In Scotland**, regulations state that prospective adopters must be given full information about a child at the time of placement, including medical information on the child and his or her birth family. **In England, Wales and Northern Ireland**, it is good practice to disclose all relevant health information to prospective adopters.

- Part C may be released in court proceedings and may be accessed by the child at a later date, so it is important to be sensitive to confidentiality and the use of language.

- Statutory guidance for England states that the lead health record for a looked after child should be the GP-held record and that the entire initial health assessment and health plan, and subsequent review assessments and plans, should be part of that record.

- Consent issues when sharing third party information need to be carefully considered in light of what is relevant to the child and in their best interests.

Part D: Data collection and audit

- This is an optional section that looked after children health teams may customise for their local data collection.

- In England, the National Tariff checklist, developed as a quality assurance tool for health assessments of children placed out of area, may be inserted here.

Form RHA–YP: review health assessment for young person 10 years and older

Purpose of the form

- To create an opportunity for discussion with the young person about their health concerns, including physical and emotional development; relationships; sexual health; possible use of tobacco, drugs and alcohol; and to encourage them to begin to assume responsibility for their own health.

- To assist young people preparing to leave care to understand their health history, assume responsibility for their own health and start to access adult health services.

- The same purposes as those of Form RHA–C.

UNDERTAKING A HEALTH ASSESSMENT

Who should complete the form?

- **Part A** should be completed by the agency/social worker.
- **Part B** should be completed by the examining health professional, either a doctor or nurse.
- **Part C** should be completed by the examining health professional.
- **Part D** may be used for data collection if desired by the responsible looked after children health team.

Guidance

All of the comments and guidance under Form RHA–C are equally applicable to Form RHA–YP, with the following specific comments.

Part A and procedure for the social worker prior to health assessment

- The social worker should make every effort to obtain informed consent for the health assessment in advance. This consent should be sought from:
  - the young person, if he or she has capacity to consent; or
  - a birth parent with parental responsibility/ies; or
  - another adult with parental responsibility/ies; or
  - an authorised representative of any agency holding parental responsibility/ies.

- With increasing maturity and understanding, it is to be expected that many, or perhaps most, young people will have capacity to consent to health assessment, and will take an increasingly active part in their own health care. If the social worker has any concerns about the young person's capacity to consent, they should seek advice from the health professional.

Part B and procedure for the assessing health professional

- There is a section for the young person to sign, giving their informed consent to the assessment. With increasing maturity and understanding, it is to be expected that many, or perhaps most, young people will have capacity to consent to a health assessment and will take an increasingly active part in their own health care.

- The emphasis should be on engaging the young person in the assessment of their own health and encouraging responsible health behaviour and a healthy lifestyle, including discussing their hopes and aspirations, rather than on completing yet another form.

- It is important to note that young people may not discuss sensitive and personal information unless confidentiality can be assured. At the outset, the issue of confidentiality should be raised with the young person and the limits of confidentiality explained. Carers or other adults should not be present during assessment unless the young person specifically gives permission. It may, however, be helpful to speak to the carer alone.

The review health assessment

- The issues raised in the report must be discussed with the young person and great care must be taken to respect confidentiality. Explicit consent for the release of personal and sensitive information to others in the health care team, carers, the school, etc, must be negotiated.

Parts C and D

See the discussion for Form RHA–C.

6 Assessment of mental health and well-being

It is essential to comprehensively consider the child's mental health and well-being at every health assessment. Utilising the prompts throughout Part B of the IHA and RHA forms in discussion with the child and their carer(s) will provide much information about the child's mental health and well-being, social and educational functioning, behaviour and resilience. This information may be enriched by use of the CoramBAAF Carers' Reports and screening tools such as the Strengths and Difficulties Questionnaire (SDQ) (Goodman, 1997). All of this information should be analysed to reach a decision about the need for further assessment or intervention.

Carers' reports

- **Form CR–C**: Carers' Report – Profile of behavioural and emotional well-being of child from birth to nine years.
- **Form CR–YP**: Carers' Report – Profile of behavioural and emotional well-being of young person aged 10–16 years.

All of the following discussion is applicable to both Forms CR–C and CR–YP.

The forms have been designed to integrate with other reports, for example, the Child's Permanence Report.

Purpose of the forms

- To provide a description of the child's or young person's emotional and behavioural well-being in the carer's own words, and to indicate change over time.
- To allow recognition of positives and flag up possible problems to assist health professionals in determining whether worrying behaviour or symptoms are present. It is NOT a diagnostic tool for mental health problems – such tools already exist. It is to be used to guide the need for further assessment and support.
- To assist adults involved with the child or young person to organise their way of thinking about them.

Assessment of mental health and well-being

- To provide information for the social worker that will give a clear and realistic picture of the child or young person, to inform important stages of their journey in care, for example, planning meetings, review meetings and placement panels, and to promote stability in placements.

- To provide an opportunity for children and young people to be involved, as appropriate for their age, in addition to receiving information from the carer.

- To form part of the child's or young person's permanent social care record. This may be accessed by a child or young person in later life and provide them with valuable information about their early home life.

Procedure for the social worker and carer prior to health assessment

- The Carers' Report should be completed by the carer(s) every time a child or young person has a statutory health assessment, or when they change placement. The child or young person should be involved in responding, as appropriate for their age and maturity. For children in a new placement, sufficient time should be allowed for the child to settle in and get to know the carer.

- The form should be completed by the main carer(s) prior to the statutory health assessment.

- Some carers may need help from their social worker to complete the form. However, the responses should reflect the carer's views.

- The completed form should be retained in the social care file.

- In thinking about the child's behaviour and emotional well-being, the carer should compare him or her to other children of similar age and ability.

- For infants under 12 months, it is only necessary to complete sections 1–5a and 9 of the form.

Procedure for the health professional at health assessment

- The voice of the carer provides invaluable information to give a rounded picture of what it is like to care for this child, his or her daily functioning and reactions to events and experiences in his or her life.

- The Carers' Report should be used alongside the comprehensive information obtained from the health assessment, including SDQ screening, to assist with analysis of emotional, mental and behavioural health and consideration of any need for further screening and interventions.

Strengths and Difficulties Questionnaire (SDQ)

The SDQ (Goodman, 1997) is a short behavioural screening questionnaire suitable for use with children and young people between the ages of four and 16 years. It has five

UNDERTAKING A HEALTH ASSESSMENT

sections covering details of emotional difficulties, conduct problems, hyperactivity or inattention, friendships and peer groups, and positive behaviour, plus an impact supplement to assist in predicting emotional health problems. It is usually completed by the parent or carer; there is a version for a teacher to complete, as well as a version for the young person to complete, if desired. The tool has been internationally validated and is appropriate for all ethnicities.

Some local authorities use the SDQ to assist in identification of children or young people who may have difficulties with mental and emotional health and who may benefit from interventions.

While there is a regional requirement to undertake screening, in **Northern Ireland** the SDQ is not routinely used. Trusts have developed their own methods of emotional health and well-being screening.

In Scotland, some areas use the SDQ; however, as this is not a requirement, other areas have developed their own screening tools.

Case examples 7

The following cases illustrate some common themes in relation to health information. Information related to the theme may be obtained from different sources and recorded on different forms and we have provided excerpts from the relevant sections/forms to demonstrate this. This is followed by the medical adviser's* analysis of the collated information (showing the adviser's thought processes) and any actions that might need to be taken. This information is shown in a box. The medical adviser then outlines this essential information in the summary and implications for the future.

The collation of information and evaluation processes will be applicable to a variety of other health issues.

CASE 1: BIRTH MOTHER WITH HISTORY OF SUBSTANCE USE

Child A is a four-month-old male. There was a pre-birth case conference as older siblings have been taken into care due to neglect; one sibling has been placed for adoption. There were concerns about the mother's ability to care for Child A. He was placed in foster care at birth and a parenting assessment has been carried out that raised significant concerns about the mother's ability to care for and safeguard him. The local authority plan is that Child A should be placed for adoption.

Relevant information will be obtained from Forms PH, M, B and IHA–C and will contribute to Part C Summary and recommendations of Form IHA–C.

---

* The analysis will most often be carried out by the medical adviser, but in some areas another health professional with the required competencies may be fulfilling this role. Throughout the case studies, the term 'medical adviser' also includes these other health professionals.

UNDERTAKING A HEALTH ASSESSMENT

Form PH on birth mother (extract)
Part B

4. Please tell me about your lifestyle

Do you or did you ever?	No	Yes – current use and quantity per day	Yes – past use and quantity per day	Used in pregnancy? At what stage?
Smoke tobacco		20 cigs/day		Reduced to 10/day
Use alcohol		Occasional use (2 pints lager per week)	Used to drink heavily (½ bottle vodka per day)	None
Use drugs: cannabis/skunk		2 smokes/day	Used to use more	Once a day in pregnancy
Heroin		Smoke occasionally (once a week)	Used to use more, including injecting until 3 years ago	Smoked heroin at the end of the pregnancy
Methadone		30mg/day	For 3 years	Throughout pregnancy
Subutex	x			
Cocaine/crack		Nil	Tried it 4 years ago	None
Amphetamines		Nil	Tried it when younger	None
Tranquillisers/ benzodiazepines	x			
Other (give names)	x			
Inject drugs		Nil	Yes – not for 3 years	No

Medical adviser's comments (Form PH) (extract)

Summary of family health issues with comments on the significance for adoption/ fostering

Birth mother smoked tobacco, cannabis and heroin during pregnancy with Child A. The mother was on the methadone (heroin replacement) programme throughout pregnancy, with regular antenatal care. Maternal serology for hepatitis B, C, HIV and syphilis should be obtained from Form M.

There is a past history of significant alcohol use. It would be useful to obtain additional information from the social worker and other sources concerning the possible continued use of alcohol in pregnancy.

Case examples

Form M (extract)
Part B

2. Substance use in this pregnancy (include duration and the trimester when used if possible)

	Provide full details
Cigarettes number/day	10 cigarettes/day in pregnancy
Alcohol units/day	Concerns about continued alcohol use in pregnancy
Other substance use (indicate if IV use, include toxicology results if available)	Smoked cannabis regularly – up to 3 times/day. Smoked heroin at least once a day. No IV drug use
Prescribed drugs	Methadone 30mg daily

3. Relevant factors in this pregnancy

		Provide full details
Gestation at booking visit	9 wks	
Was regular antenatal care given?	Yes	Specialist midwifery team
Domestic violence	No	Suspected past history
Evidence of foetal growth retardation	Yes	Monitored with ultrasound scans
Abnormal ultrasound	No	
Amniocentesis	No	
Medical illness in pregnancy	No	
Drug treatment in pregnancy	Yes	Methadone 30mg daily as stated
Mental illness/depression in pregnancy	No	
Genetic illness in extended family	No	

4. Maternal blood tests

	Result	Date/s
Hepatitis B	Negative	9 weeks gestation, at booking visit *
Hepatitis C	Negative	9 weeks gestation, at booking visit *
HIV	Negative	9 weeks gestation, at booking visit *
Syphilis	Negative	9 weeks gestation, at booking visit *
Other		

*Normally the date of testing would be provided here, but we have used descriptive terms for illustration purposes.

UNDERTAKING A HEALTH ASSESSMENT

Form B (extract)
Part B

5. Postnatal period

Condition	Yes/No	Details of condition and treatment
Feeding		Breast or bottle, feeding difficulties Mother breast fed initially. Baby established on formula feeds prior to discharge
Jaundice	No	Include maximum bilirubin and duration of treatment
Symptomatic hypoglycaemia	No	Include duration and lowest level
Neonatal withdrawal syndrome	Yes	Include maximum score and treatment details Monitored for withdrawal symptoms. Maximum Lipsitz score 2 out of 20. No treatment required
Respiratory distress	No	Include details of ventilation
Infection	No	
Seizures	No	
Others		

6. Were there any abnormalities on neonatal examination? If yes, provide full details

Neonatal examination satisfactory. Newborn hearing screening satisfactory both ears.

7. Any concerns or observations about the mother's relationship with the baby

The mother was encouraged to breast feed to ameliorate possible effects of withdrawal. The mother cared for the baby with support from nursing staff. No concerns noted.

Note: The medical adviser's comments relating to Form B are included in the Summary on Form IHA–C.

Form IHA–C (extract)
Part B

1. Health discussion

Is the child currently well? Does the child or carer have any concerns about the child's health or well-being, e.g. eating, sleeping, development, school, behaviour? Does anyone else involved with the child have any concerns?

Child A was placed at three days of age. The foster carer was concerned about jitteriness, sneezing, excessive crying and difficulties in feeding for the first six weeks. Seen by GP and paediatric assessment unit but no treatment required.

The foster carer noted that Child A was late to smile, achieving this at nine weeks. The GP referred the child to the ophthalmologist, who thought that the child had experienced delayed visual maturation which had now resolved.

Case examples

> **Medical adviser's analysis and actions**
>
> **This section is included to illustrate how the medical adviser will analyse the information obtained thus far and consider whether further action is needed to confirm the information provided or to obtain additional information.**
>
> The social worker had helped the birth mother complete Form PH comprehensively, providing as much information as possible.
>
> Forms M and B confirmed maternal use of tobacco, alcohol, cannabis and heroin, as well as prescribed methadone. Maternal serology for hepatitis B, C, HIV and syphilis was negative during pregnancy. The medical adviser contacted the midwifery team who knew the birth mother well. Serology was not repeated at delivery as antenatal care was regular and the mother was known to smoke heroin and cannabis and regular methadone prescriptions were given. The mother is known to be needle phobic and there was no evidence of IV use. Continued concerns about maternal alcohol use during pregnancy were confirmed by the social worker.
>
> Although Child A was monitored for withdrawal symptoms for 72 hours prior to discharge, these symptoms were not significant and no treatment was required. However, at the initial health assessment the foster carer gave a history of jitteriness, excessive crying and irritability in the first six weeks of life. The child was also late to smile and had delayed visual maturation. These signs and symptoms are likely to be related to withdrawal from maternal methadone.

Form IHA–C (extract)

Part C Summary and implications for future (extract)

Child A's mother used tobacco, cannabis, heroin and methadone (heroin replacement) during pregnancy. It is also likely that the mother drank alcohol in pregnancy. The child has no physical features of FAS but suffered from withdrawal symptoms from methadone and/or heroin in the early weeks. Antenatal substance exposure has implications for Child A and means he is at risk of developmental concerns at any stage of development. Other than delayed visual maturation, now resolved, Child A's development is age-appropriate at this time. However, as Child A is only four months of age, it is difficult to predict future health and development with any degree of accuracy and potential carers should be aware of this.

UNDERTAKING A HEALTH ASSESSMENT

CASE 2: BIRTH MOTHER WITH HISTORY OF PHYSICAL AND MENTAL HEALTH CONDITIONS

Child B is an 11-year-old female who came into care when her birth mother, who is a single parent, was hospitalised with an acute episode of schizophrenia.

Form PH on birth mother (extract)
Part B

2. Personal health history (abstract)

Have you ever suffered from or been treated for any of the following?

(Please indicate yes/no and give details)

Note: for clarity, only the conditions marked yes are listed below.

	Yes	No	Details
Asthma/bronchitis or chest problems	Yes		Regular daily use of inhaler
(N/A)			
Skin conditions	Yes		Eczema as a child
(N/A)			
Depression	Yes		Bipolar
Anxiety	Yes		All the time
Emotional problems	Yes		Since a teenager
Other mental health diagnosis	Yes		Schizophrenia
Other			

7. Family history (abstract)

Please tell me about the health of your family. Does anyone have any serious health problems, such as those listed in section 2? Does anyone have any genetic conditions that may run in the family?

	Age now	State of health if living	Cause of, and age at death
Father	60	Mental health problems (Schizophrenia?)	
Mother	55	Asthma. Smokes heavily. Suffers with her nerves	
Your brothers and sisters	Dan 29 Pete 25	OK ADHD, asthma	

Case examples

Medical adviser's comments (Form PH) (extract)

Summary of family health issues with comments on the significance for adoption/fostering

Birth mother has a diagnosis of schizophrenia and bipolar disorder, and confirmation from psychiatrist and GP is needed. Child B's maternal grandfather is believed to have schizophrenia but this has not been confirmed.

Birth mother suffers from asthma and there is a family history of asthma in Child B's maternal uncle and maternal grandmother. Child B's maternal uncle is believed to have ADHD but this has not been confirmed.

Medical adviser's analysis and actions

This section is included to illustrate how the medical adviser will analyse the information obtained thus far and consider whether further action is needed to confirm the information provided or to obtain additional information.

The social worker had helped the birth mother to complete Form PH comprehensively, providing as much information as possible.

The medical adviser contacted the GP to clarify the diagnoses of schizophrenia and bipolar disorder in the birth mother. The GP confirmed a diagnosis of schizophrenia and attached a letter from the psychiatrist. There is no past or present diagnosis of bipolar affective disorder but reactive depression in the past is documented in GP records. The GP confirmed the history of asthma and eczema.

Information from the birth mother indicates that the grandfather may have schizophrenia and the uncle may have ADHD but this third party information cannot readily be confirmed.

Form IHA–YP

Part C Summary and implications for future (extract)

Child B's mother has schizophrenia. There is also a possible diagnosis of schizophrenia in the maternal grandfather. Child B is at increased risk of developing schizophrenia and potential carers should be aware of this.

A maternal uncle is believed to have ADHD. This cannot be confirmed but prospective carers should be aware of this information.

There is a family history of asthma and eczema. Child B suffers from asthma, which has improved over the last two years.

UNDERTAKING A HEALTH ASSESSMENT

CASE 3: BIRTH FATHER WITH LEARNING DIFFICULTIES AND FAMILY HISTORY OF HEART DISEASE

Child C is a three-year-old female who came into care following concerns about parenting and possible non-accidental injury.

Form PH on birth father (extract)
Part B

6. Do you have or have you ever had problems with:

Reading	Yes
Writing, or filling in forms	Yes
Spelling	Yes
Using numbers	Yes
Speech and language, including autism or Asperger's	No
Concentration and attention/ADHD/hyperactivity	Yes – find it hard to concentrate for long periods

Did you receive extra support in school?   Yes

Did you attend a special school/unit? Give reason, e.g. behaviour, learning difficulties, other

Yes – learning difficulties – special school

7. Family history

Please tell me about the health of your family. Does anyone have any serious health problems, such as those listed in section 2? Does anyone have any genetic conditions that may run in the family?

	Age now	State of health if living	Cause of, and age at death
Father			Died of heart attack age 42 (heavy smoker)
Mother	52	Healthy	
Your brothers and sisters	Adam 17 Mary 22	Healthy – difficult behaviour Healthy	
Your children			
Other			

Has anyone in your family, either now, or in the past, had:	State their relationship to you and give details of their difficulty
Learning difficulties	My mother and auntie and brother, Adam
Reading/writing difficulties	Yes, Mum and Auntie and brother, Adam
Special schooling	Yes, I think so
Mental health problems: please specify, e.g. drug or alcohol dependency, suicide, depression	Mum depressed since Dad died

Form IHA–C

1. Health discussion

Is the child currently well? Does the child or carer have any concerns about the child's health or well-being, e.g. eating, sleeping, development, school, behaviour? Does anyone else involved with the child have any concerns?

The foster carer has been concerned about development since the child was placed. Considerable progress has been made in all areas of development but some difficulties remain with speech and language.

9. Developmental/functional assessment (Record age-appropriate activities to document skills)

Note: For clarity, only the relevant section of the development assessment is included here.

Date and results of any formal developmental assessment e.g. SOGS (schedule of growing skills), Ruth Griffiths, Bayley, ASQ (ages and stages questionnaire)

Recent schedule of growing skills completed by the health visitor shows delay in gross motor skills and speech and language development (this should be attached to the IHA–C report). The health visitor has referred the child to a speech and language therapist and will continue to monitor development.

UNDERTAKING A HEALTH ASSESSMENT

> **Medical adviser's analysis and actions**
>
> **This section is included to illustrate how the medical adviser will analyse the information obtained thus far and consider whether further action is needed to confirm the information provided or to obtain additional information.**
>
> Birth father provided information verbally while the social worker filled in the form for him, enabling comprehensive completion of Form PH. The social worker knew the family well and was able to confirm the presence of learning difficulties in other family members.
>
> Paternal grandfather was known to smoke heavily and is understood to have died from a heart attack at an early age. Because of the potential risk to Child C of cardiovascular disease, it is important to confirm cause of death by requesting that the social worker obtain the paternal grandfather's death certificate. This confirmed death from a heart attack at age 42.
>
> Child C has made progress developmentally since entering foster care. A recent SOGS shows delay in gross motor skills and speech and language, and it is important that the health visitor should continue to monitor this.

Part C Summary and implications for future (extract)

Child C has some evidence of developmental delay but has made good progress since entering foster care. Gross motor skills and speech and language development remain a concern. This may be attributed to lack of stimulation but Child C is at increased risk given the paternal family history of learning difficulties. Potential carers should be aware of this risk and the need for continued monitoring.

Paternal grandfather died from a heart attack aged 42. There may be an inherited risk of heart disease and therefore monitoring and investigations should be considered before adulthood, as well as advice on lifestyle. Potential carers and the GP should be made aware of this information.

Health recommendations for child care plan

Health issues	Action required	By when	Person responsible
Routine child health and school health surveillance		At appropriate times	Carer Health visitor GP and school nurse
Family history of learning difficulties	Monitoring and awareness in school setting	Ongoing	Carer Social worker School
Family history of cardiovascular problems	Information to be shared with agency, GP and carers	Immediately	Medical adviser

Adult health assessment 8

This chapter discusses CoramBAAF Forms AH and AH2, which are used to assess adult health. Form AH is used to record the comprehensive health assessment carried out on all prospective substitute carers when they first apply. Form AH2 is used at periodic intervals to undertake a review of the health of foster carers and those approved adopters who have not yet had a child placed. CoramBAAF will be developing a new Form AH Review for use in reviewing the health of approved foster carers.*

Purpose of the adult health assessment

The aim of substitute care is to provide disadvantaged children with nurturing carers and secure, stable placements lasting as long as a child needs them. Carers need to have robust physical and mental health to be able to cope readily with parenting these vulnerable and sometimes challenging children. A comprehensive health assessment should be carried out for all foster carers, kinship carers, special guardians and adopters to assist agencies in understanding the level of health risk that must be considered alongside a range of other factors in order to reach a decision about approval.

Medical advisers, panels and decision-makers should apply the same health standards for foster carers and adopters, but agencies may decide to accept a higher level of health risk for placements with kinship carers and special guardians if there are clearly identified benefits of the placement for specific children.

The primary purpose of the adult health assessment and medical adviser's advice is to inform the assessing social worker of any health issues that may need to be explored in the social work assessment of the prospective foster carer(s) or adoptive parent(s), and to advise the agency and panel about health risks. Individual consideration must be given to the health of each applicant.

---

* Information about any new forms will be publicised via *CoramBAAF News*.

> **Guiding principles when considering difficult health issues in adults who wish to care for children (Mather and Lehner, 2010)**
>
> - *The welfare of the child is paramount.*
> - *Parenting capacities are more important than perfect health.*
> - *Honesty and openness in dealing with applicants are essential.*

Legal and statutory duties

Prospective adopters

Regulations throughout the UK* require that the adoption agency obtain a report prepared by a fully registered medical practitioner following a full examination (unless the medical adviser deems it unnecessary) as to the health of each person proposing to adopt a child. **In Wales**, the health assessment must be completed no more than six months prior to the panel.

The Prospective Adopter's Report (or equivalent) should include a summary of the state of health of the prospective adopters, written by the medical adviser. In terms of evaluating the health of prospective adopters, the statutory involvement of the medical adviser ceases when the adoption order is granted. Further involvement is at the discretion of the prospective adopters and will depend on each service agreement between NHS trusts and the agency. Clearly, however, in some situations it is good practice for the medical adviser to continue his or her involvement.

Adoption in England

New applicants

As a result of the Government's intention to recruit more adopters and speed up the approval process, a two-stage adopter approval process came into effect in England from July 2013. During Stage 1, described as the pre-assessment process, the prospective adopter learns about adoption through preparation groups, relevant reading, and exploration of the issues with support from the agency, while the agency carries out the required statutory checks, including references and the health assessment. While Stage 1 should normally be completed within two months, there is recognition that this may take longer, for instance, when applicants need more time or in order to obtain comprehensive health information. At the end of Stage 1, the agency will decide whether the applicants can proceed to Stage 2 based on the outcome of all the statutory checks. The applicants then decide when they are ready to start Stage 2; they can take up to a six-month break between the two stages.

---

* The Adoption Agencies Regulations 2005 (England), Adoption Agencies (Wales) Regulations 2005, Adoption Agencies Regulations (Northern Ireland) 1989 and Adoption Agencies (Scotland) Regulations 2009.

If the applicant and agency decide to proceed, then Stage 2 will involve a detailed assessment culminating in a comprehensive Prospective Adopter's Report (PAR) to be considered by the adoption panel. It is expected that the agency decision-maker will make the decision about approval within four months of the commencement of Stage 2.

Fast-track process

A fast-track process has been introduced for adopters who have previously adopted in a court in England or Wales after having been approved under the Adoption Agencies Regulations 2005 (or corresponding Welsh provision), or intercountry adopters who have been assessed under the Adoptions with a Foreign Element Regulations 2005, and anyone who is a fully approved foster carer in England at the time they apply to adopt. It is important that the social worker works with the medical adviser to determine what is needed, as the Statutory Guidance gives responsibility to the medical adviser to decide whether a full or update report is required:

> *The agency must obtain a written report from a registered medical practitioner about the health of the prospective adopter following a full examination. The report must include the matters specified in Part 2, Schedule 4 of the AAR, **unless** the agency has received advice from its medical adviser that such an examination and report is unnecessary.*

> *Agencies will in each individual case need to determine whether prescribed checks and/or references should be sought depending on the time since approval and, in the case of foster carers, the time since a child was placed with them. Agencies are required to complete the fast-track process within four months.*

> (DfE, Statutory Adoption Guidance, 2013)

Adoption in Wales and Northern Ireland

Some adoption agencies require all the statutory checks, including the health assessment, to be undertaken before the assessment begins, whilst others undertake checks and assessment concurrently. The comprehensive report prepared in Wales is called the Prospective Adopter's Report (PAR Wales) and in Northern Ireland the Form F (Adoption and Permanence Northern Ireland) is used. The whole process should take no longer than eight months.

Adoption in Scotland

In Scotland, the processes for assessment of prospective adopters are set out in the Adoption Agencies (Scotland) Regulations 2009, particularly regulation 7 and Schedule 1, Part I. Every agency has to have general criteria for deciding whether people may be accepted as applicants. If applicants are accepted for assessment, the agency must gather a wide range of information, assess the case, prepare a report and then refer the applicants to its adoption panel. The information to be gathered includes 'a comprehensive medical report on the prospective adopter prepared and signed by a registered medical practitioner including such details as the medical adviser to the panel considers necessary in the circumstance' (Schedule 1 Part I, paragraph 25). The report should include information about the applicant's personality (paragraph 12) and an assessment of his or her 'ability to raise an adopted child throughout their childhood' (paragraph 15). The 2007 Act Guidance states that:

> This directs attention in the assessment to the whole period of a child's dependency and their transition to adulthood. Factors such as age and health may be relevant here. It is important to recognise however that circumstances change in families and that adoption support services have a role to play when these changes occur.
>
> (Scottish Government, 2011, Chapter 19.4)

Prospective foster carers

The Fostering Services (England) Regulations 2011, the Fostering Services (Wales) Regulations 2003, the *Children (Northern Ireland) Order 1995 Guidance and Regulations: Volume 3, Family Placements and Private Fostering*, and the Looked After Children (Scotland) Regulations 2009 require details of the prospective foster carer's health, supported by a medical report. Use of the CoramBAAF adult health assessment Form AH provides a comprehensive assessment for fostering applicants, and CoramBAAF's Health Group Advisory Committee strongly recommends that the agency medical adviser should review the form and advise on health risk.

Fostering in England

From July 2013, a two-stage process for assessing fostering applicants came into effect in England. Stage 1 encompasses various checks including the health assessment, although this may be extended, for instance, when additional time is required to obtain comprehensive health information. The Fostering Regulations require agencies to reach a decision about suitability to move to Stage 2 of the assessment within 10 days of receiving all of the Stage 1 information. As the timescales do not impose requirements on the medical practitioners, the agency should consider receipt of the health assessment report from the agency medical adviser to be the start of the 10-day period, if that is the final piece of information that is awaited. There is no specified duration for Stage 1 or 2 for fostering applicants, but the whole assessment process should be completed within eight months.

Fostering and kinship care in Scotland

In Scotland, the processes for assessment of prospective foster carers are set out in the Looked After Children (Scotland) Regulations 2009, particularly regulations 21 and 22 and Schedule 3. Assessments of prospective kinship carers for looked after children are set out in regulation 10 and Schedule 3, so the same information is required for both groups of applicants.

For assessment of foster carers, the local authority or agency must gather a wide range of information, prepare a report and then refer the applicants to their fostering panel. The information to be gathered includes details about their health, supported by a medical report (Schedule 3, paragraph 1). The Guidance states that certain checks, including health ones, should be undertaken early in the process if it is thought that there may be 'contentious or problematic issues' (Scottish Government, 2011, Chapter 11.1). The recommended time for the whole assessment is six months (Chapter 11.7).

The Guidance continues:

> The applicants should be informed that they will be required to have a full medical examination. Application forms ask for information about their GP. The role of the medical adviser to the panel should be explained. Where there are any health issues, these could mean that the medical adviser may need to seek further information from any specialist consultant who was or continues to be involved. Applicants should also be aware from the outset about authorities' policy on smoking, covering both age restrictions on children who can be placed if there is a smoker in the household; and also the broader local authority view of the importance of a smoke-free environment for children, and modelling healthy lifestyles. These issues may broaden to include any local authority policies on other lifestyle issues.

(Chapter 11.5)

For assessment of kinship carers, the local authority must gather the same wide range of information and prepare a report. The information includes details about the applicants' health, supported by a medical report (Schedule 3, paragraph 1). Kinship carer applications are not required to be considered by a panel, although some local authorities do refer them to a fostering or other panel. Kinship care is covered by Chapter 9 of the Guidance (Scottish Government, 2011).

Prospective special guardians in England and Wales

The Special Guardianship Regulations 2005 form part of the legal framework for special guardianship orders in England. The special guardianship report to the court must include a health history of the prospective special guardian, including details of any serious physical and mental health illnesses, any hereditary disease or disorder or disability (Special Guardianship Regulations 2005), and also a summary prepared by the medical professional who provided the information. The Special Guardianship (Wales) Regulations 2005 require a similar health report. The CoramBAAF Health Group Advisory Committee recommends the use of CoramBAAF Form AH for this assessment.

There are no provisions for special guardianship in Northern Ireland or Scotland.

Medical adviser for adoption

Regulation 3(1)(b) of the Adoption Agencies and Independent Review of Determinations (Amendment) Regulations 2011 requires an agency in England to include on its central list the medical adviser to the adoption agency (or at least one if more than one medical adviser is appointed) (Lord and Cullen, 2016). Regulation 3(1)(b) of the Adoption Agencies (Wales) Regulations 2005, as amended in 2014, requires the same of an agency in Wales. Regulation 6 of the Adoption Agencies Regulations (Northern Ireland) 1989 requires the adoption agency to nominate a medical practitioner to be the agency's medical adviser. Regulation 5 of the Adoption Agencies (Scotland) Regulations 2009 requires all agencies to appoint as many medical advisers as they consider necessary, and advisers must be registered medical practitioners. Every adoption panel must include a medical adviser (regulation 3(4)(a)).

It is recommended that agencies make arrangements for the appointment of a medical adviser with a local Health Trust/Health Board's designated doctor for looked after children.

Medical adviser for fostering

In England, Wales and Northern Ireland, there is no statutory requirement for a medical adviser to be appointed as a member of a fostering panel, but the panel must have access to medical advice if required. **In Scotland**, local authorities and fostering services are required to appoint as many medical advisers as they consider necessary to provide their fostering panels with medical advice, and these must be registered medical practitioners (regulation 19(1) and (3), Looked After Children (Scotland) Regulations 2009). Every fostering panel must include a medical adviser (regulation 17(4)).

CoramBAAF's Health Group Advisory Committee recommends as good practice that a medical adviser should review all health assessments on prospective carers, provide written advice and attend the panel. In some areas, specialist nurses for looked after children sit on fostering panels and may be well placed to advise on health concerns for looked after children, but they may not be able to comment on adult health issues.

Where medical issues are being considered, it is essential that supervising social workers and other non-medical professionals take advice from qualified and registered medical practitioners. It is not appropriate for non-medical staff to interpret medical information without such advice and guidance. Neither is it appropriate to expect medical practitioners to make decisions about suitability to foster; there are clear processes for this, and health information needs to be seen as part of a wider picture.

Health reviews

Foster carers will require regular health reviews as part of the review process, and likewise those prospective adopters who have not yet had a child placed will also require a review.

Adopters

Regulation 29 of the England Adoption Agency Regulations 2005, regulation 30 of the Adoption Agencies (Wales) Regulations 2005, and the Northern Ireland Adoption Regional Policy and Procedures 2010 require the agency to review prospective adopters' approval periodically until a child is placed for adoption with them or a match is under active consideration. This review must be held in England and Northern Ireland a year after approval and then at yearly intervals; two years after approval and thereafter two-yearly in Wales, or earlier if the agency considers it necessary, for instance, if a couple separates or there are substantive changes in health.

In Scotland, an adoption agency is required to review approval of adopters in certain circumstances. These are that either no child has been placed with the adopters within two years of approval, or a child has been placed but there has been no application to court and the agency thinks that a review is needed 'to safeguard or promote the welfare of the child' (regulation 10(2) or (3), Adoption Agencies (Scotland) Regulations 2009).

At such reviews, prospective adopters should be asked whether there has been any change in health since their previous health assessment. The agency medical adviser should be consulted as to whether it is necessary to obtain further information or carry out a comprehensive assessment. CoramBAAF Form AH2, which was designed to provide an update from records of information on Form AH, may be used if further information is needed.

Foster carers

There are no specific statutory requirements to review the health of foster carers, although there are provisions across the UK for a range of reviews of continuing approval. Agency practice has varied. Historically, the BAAF (now CoramBAAF) Health Group Advisory Committee has recommended that foster carers should have routine health reviews at two-yearly intervals, alternating between a comprehensive health assessment necessitating a visit to their GP (using Form AH), and a request for information from the carers and their GP (using Form AH2). However, this approach overlooked the importance of ongoing monitoring and support regarding health concerns of carers, and tended to place the responsibility for health matters on health professionals rather than social care practitioners.

Scottish Guidance (Chapter 12.4, Scottish Government, 2011) states that any significant change, including a foster carer's ill health, may require an early review. Chapter 12.9 states that:

> *For medical checks, there should be a medical update as part of every annual review, considered along with the original medical assessment. In addition, and as a minimum, a full health assessment should be carried out again at the second three year review, i.e. the seven year review; and thereafter every six years. A full health assessment should also be carried out when circumstances indicate this is needed; or when there is to be a significant change in the carer's remit; or when there are significant health concerns.*

The CoramBAAF Health Group Advisory Committee and social care colleagues have recently been considering more collaborative approaches to monitoring health that meet legal and good practice requirements. In managing health issues of foster carers, there are a number of principles that should inform practice:

- All prospective foster carers should be subject to the comprehensive health assessment process, including advice from a medical adviser, as previously discussed.

- Foster carers should understand that it is their responsibility to inform their supervising social worker (or other member of the fostering service) about any changes to their health that might impact on their ability to foster, or might be perceived as likely to impact on their fostering.

- Similarly, supervising social workers should recognise that they have a responsibility to talk to foster carers about their health, and to raise any issues based on observations or other information provided to them. Best practice suggests that these discussions should take place in the context of a good professional relationship where the foster carer feels valued and supported.

UNDERTAKING A HEALTH ASSESSMENT

- The foster carer review should also consider the matter of the foster carer's health, and the foster carer and supervising social worker should be asked to comment on this. The fostering service might wish to consider the use of an annual health questionnaire (in the future, CoramBAAF will publish a new Form AH Review developed by the Health Group Advisory Committee).*

- Where medical issues are identified at a review, it is essential that non-medical professionals take advice from a medical adviser.

- When questions or concerns arise about health, there should always be an opportunity to seek further information from the foster carer's GP, relevant consultant or other qualified medical practitioner, to assess risks to health and parenting ability. Fostering services need to be reassured that foster carers are sufficiently healthy to undertake the fostering task, and to have information that allows them to effectively support the carer. At times, the medical adviser may recommend that a comprehensive health assessment be completed (using Form AH); this should not be perceived as criticism of the foster carer, and there should be an expectation that foster carers comply with this request where it is reasonably made.

- In cases where there is doubt or disagreement about the significance of health concerns, services should err on the side of caution and require that a more detailed assessment be undertaken, or a named consultant be contacted. A robust safeguarding approach should be taken that recognises that fostering services need good information about the health of their foster carers.

- If at any point a condition is identified that could impair the carer's ability to care safely, then in addition to ongoing monitoring by the social worker, medical advice should be sought concerning how and when to conduct the next review of the carer's health.

- Fostering services should recognise that periods of ill health are the norm for many parents and carers, and wherever possible should look at how best to support foster carers in such circumstances. Any supportive arrangements must take account of the needs of any children placed, and should consider the likely prognosis and timescales in each individual set of circumstances.

- Fostering services should promote healthy lifestyles, ensuring that foster carers are provided with relevant information about smoking, alcohol use, diet, exercise, obesity and stress management.

- A comprehensive health assessment with the carer's usual GP at regular intervals is a helpful part of a wider strategy, and the CoramBAAF Health Group Advisory Committee recommends that they occur at least every five years.

Form AH2 was designed to provide an update from records of information on Form AH. In view of the above recommendations, Form AH2 will be phased out for fostering, and a health questionnaire (Form AH Review) for use at the annual review will be developed by the CoramBAAF Health Group Advisory Committee. *

---

* Information about any new forms will be publicised via *CoramBAAF News*.

Form AH: adult health assessment process and documentation

Form AH is recommended as the basis of the assessment and provides standardisation throughout the UK. This form is used for an initial health assessment on applicants for fostering, adoption, intercountry adoption, kinship care, special guardianship, and short break/respite care.

Purpose of the form

- To obtain, based on health history, medical examination and health information from records, an up-to-date, comprehensive and accurate report on the applicant's individual and family health history and current physical, emotional and mental health, including lifestyle factors that may have an impact on their ability to parent a vulnerable child.

- To assist the agency or service in assessing health and lifestyle risk factors that may affect the decision regarding the applicant's suitability to care for a child.

Who should complete the form?

- **Part A** should be completed by the agency and the entire form given to the applicant.

- **Part B** should be completed by the applicant and the entire form given to their GP.

- **Part C** should be completed by the applicant's own GP, unless special circumstances indicate that another doctor has better knowledge, and the entire completed form sent to the agency medical adviser.

Part A and procedure for the agency/local authority

- Part A contains the information that identifies the agency, indicates the type of substitute care role for which the applicant is applying, and should be completed in full by the agency.

- To protect confidentiality, the GP should send the form directly to the agency medical adviser and the agency should ensure that the name and address of the medical adviser are stated correctly. It is a breach of confidentiality if the form is sent to other agencies such as CoramBAAF.

- The agency should prepare the applicant for the assessment, explaining that carers will need to have robust physical and mental health to be able to parent vulnerable children who have experienced trauma and loss. The impact on parenting of specific medical factors and health-related lifestyle factors such as smoking, alcohol consumption, gross obesity, diet and exercise will need to be considered.

- The agency should explain that the applicant will be asked to give their consent to access their health history, have an examination by and report from their GP, and for further enquiries to be made by the medical adviser if necessary.

- The social worker should explain agency policy concerning confidentiality and information sharing so that the applicant understands that while the details of their health will be kept confidential to the medical adviser, a summary of all relevant health and lifestyle information will be shared within the agency on a need to know basis and shared in written assessment reports provided for fostering and adoption panels. The health summary may be shared with the child's agency at the time of placement.

- In the case of a couple, the social worker should explain that the information regarding one applicant is confidential to that applicant and this confidentiality will be respected.

- Applicants should be made aware that they have an ongoing responsibility to inform the agency of any significant changes to their health so that the agency can consult with the medical adviser and consider the implications on their capacity to care for a child.

- Once Part A is completed, the agency should give it to the applicant, who will complete Part B and arrange an assessment with their usual GP, unless another doctor has better knowledge of the applicant for a particular reason.

- The agency should send a commissioning letter signed by the agency medical adviser to the GP, explaining the reason for the assessment and briefly outlining the challenges of parenting children with complex needs and difficult behaviour. The agency should offer a suitable fee to the GP, indicate where to send the completed form and account, and ensure prompt payment on receipt of the comprehensively completed form.

Part B and procedure for the social worker and applicant

- Having been prepared by the social worker, the applicant should sign the consent form, indicating that they understand the purpose of the assessment, and consent to the agency obtaining their health information.

- The applicant should answer all of the questions, providing as much detail as possible.

- The applicant should then sign a statement indicating that the information provided is complete and accurate.

- The applicant should then give the form to their GP for completion at the health assessment.

Part C and procedure for the GP

- The applicant's GP must acknowledge that they have reviewed the information provided by the applicant and add any relevant comments or recommendations.

- The GP is requested to provide accurate and up-to-date information, based on the medical examination and medical facts from records, on the applicant's individual and family health history and current physical and mental health. The GP is not required to make a decision on suitability, but rather to provide sufficient accurate and detailed information to enable the medical adviser to advise the agency on health risk when considering the applicant's suitability to care for a child.

Adult health assessment

- The GP should complete the form, providing detailed information wherever relevant. The GP may wish to include relevant reports with the form when returning it to the agency medical examiner.

Interpretation of Form AH by the agency medical adviser

- The agency medical adviser should take account of medical history, current health and health-related lifestyle factors and evaluate these carefully to provide advice to the agency on the implications for the applicant's health. The impact of health conditions on activities of daily living may be more important than the condition itself.

- The medical adviser should have undergone higher professional training in paediatrics and be competent to at least Level 3 of the Intercollegiate Competencies.

- The role of medical advisers for VAAs and IFPs, that largely recruit adult carers, may be undertaken by a GP with expertise or other registered medical practitioner who has relevant specialist training. However, they should have knowledge and expertise of children with very complex needs, as these agencies are likely to be recruiting carers for such children, and competence to Level 3 of the Intercollegiate Competencies.

- The agency medical adviser should be well informed about the implications for adoption and fostering of a variety of factors, including chronic conditions, treated cancer and psychiatric history. For adoptive applicants, current treatment for infertility, the implications of infertility and perinatal loss will need consideration, so full details, including termination of pregnancy, should be provided. For discussion of particular conditions, see Merredew and Sampeys, 2015.

- After review of the information provided in Form AH, it may be necessary to obtain additional written information from any consultant who has been responsible for the patient's care. Additional written permission to do this should be obtained from the applicant, as the consent on Form AH is inadequate for further enquiries. Applicants should be reassured that such information will be dealt with in the strictest confidence and will be used only to inform the process of assessment.

- In these cases, it is advisable to ask the consultant, in writing, very specific questions, including the impact of the condition on daily functioning, the short- and long-term prognosis and the chance of a prolonged period of debilitating illness. It is also important to ensure that the consultant understands the need for robust physical and mental health to parent a child with complex needs, and the need for applicants to have a reasonable probability of being able to parent a child until adulthood.

- Some medical advisers copy their letter to the consultant to the applicant and to the GP, indicating to the consultant that they have done so. An example of a request for further written information is provided overleaf.

- The medical adviser is required to prepare a summary on the prospective carer's or adopter's health, which forms part of the report for the panel. This summary should take account of medical history, current health and health-related lifestyle issues.

UNDERTAKING A HEALTH ASSESSMENT

> **Example of letter to consultant requesting additional information**
>
> Dear Dr_____
>
> **Re:** **Name:**
>
> **DoB:**
>
> **Address:**
>
> I write as medical adviser to........adoption and permanency/fostering panel. Your previous patient has applied to be an adopter/foster carer/special guardian. I have permission to contact you and a copy of the consent is attached.
>
> Carers are urgently required for children of different ages and with differing needs. Carers need to be mentally and physically robust and, for long-term placements, to have a reasonable expectation of being able to care for the child into adult life. In making a recommendation about their suitability, the panel will focus solely on the needs of the children.
>
> We have been informed that the above named person has a significant medical condition. I would be grateful for further details of the following:
>
> 1. Presentation of episodes; in particular, did they involve any risk to him/herself or others at the time?
>
> 2. Compliance and response to treatment.
>
> 3. Impact on daily activities.
>
> 4. Long-term prognosis.
>
> I would appreciate a reply as soon as possible to prevent delay to the application. Please note that your reply may be copied to both your patient and the assessing social worker.
>
> Yours sincerely
>
> Medical adviser

Interagency working between the medical adviser and social worker/agency

- The medical adviser should share concerns about health risk with the assessing social worker so that these can be sensitively and comprehensively explored with the applicant(s). This provides the applicant(s) with an important opportunity to reflect on how they would meet the needs of a child in various difficult scenarios, including prolonged and demanding ill-health or even premature death. Support systems, coping strategies and potential need for placement support should all be considered.

- In most cases, it is a couple, not an individual, who come forward to be considered as carers. Social workers and medical advisers need to carefully consider the illogical situation of rejecting a healthy, well-motivated applicant because of health problems in their partner. Where one applicant has significant health risks, the assessment must focus on the motivation and abilities of both partners and their support networks. The social worker will need to weigh up the potential impact of declining health in one partner on the capacity of the other to cope with their partner's illness. There will also be an unpredictable impact on the carer's birth children and any other children in placement, which needs to be carefully considered.

- Assessing an applicant's mental health may involve consultation with an adult psychiatrist and close liaison with the social worker assessing the case, who will have further information gained from the applicant and from interviews with referees. As with any health issue, this needs careful assessment and liaison with adult specialists and social workers for further information.

- Medical advisers and social workers need to remember that applicants whose application is turned down by an agency have a right to know on what grounds they were rejected. Hence, doctors and social workers should be scrupulously open and honest from the beginning.

Health review

Foster carers will require regular health reviews as part of the review process, and likewise those prospective adopters who have not yet had a child placed will also require a review. As previously stated, Form AH2 may be used for adoption if further information is needed, and may be used for foster carer reviews until CoramBAAF's new Form AH Review is developed for use as part of the annual foster carer review.*

Form AH2: update adult health report

This form should **not** be used where the applicant has health problems that have implications for the care of the child, or where the original Form AH indicated areas of concern. In these situations, a comprehensive health assessment should be carried out using Form AH.

Purpose of the form

- To update from records the information recorded on Form AH.

Who should complete the form?

- **Part A** should be completed by the agency and the entire form given to the applicant.

---

* Information about any new forms will be publicised via *CoramBAAF News*.

UNDERTAKING A HEALTH ASSESSMENT

- **Part B** should be completed by the applicant and the entire form given to their GP.
- **Part C** should be completed by the GP and the entire form sent to the agency medical adviser named in Part A.

Part A and procedure for the agency/local authority

- Part A contains the information that identifies the agency, indicates the type of substitute care role for which the applicant is applying, and should be completed in full by the agency.

- To protect confidentiality, the GP should send the form directly to the agency medical adviser and the agency should ensure that the name and address of the medical adviser are stated correctly. It is a breach of confidentiality if the form is sent to other agencies such as CoramBAAF.

- The agency should prepare the applicant for the assessment, explaining that they will be asked to give consent to share health information, and to provide up-to-date information about their health and lifestyle by completing Part B in advance of the form being sent to the GP to complete.

- Completion of this form provides an opportunity for the agency to stress that the applicant or carer has an ongoing responsibility to inform the agency of any significant changes to their health, so that the agency can consult with the medical adviser and consider the implications on their capacity to care for a child.

- Once Part A is completed, the agency should give it to the applicant, who will complete Part B.

- The agency should send a commissioning letter signed by the agency medical adviser to the GP, explaining the requirement for updated information and briefly outlining the challenges of parenting children with complex needs and difficult behaviour. The agency should offer a suitable fee to the GP, indicate where to send the completed form and account, and ensure prompt payment on receipt of the comprehensively completed form.

Part B and procedure for the social worker and applicant

- Having been prepared by the social worker, the applicant should sign the consent form, indicating that they understand the purpose of the report, and consent to the agency obtaining their health information.

- The applicant should answer all of the questions, providing as much detail as possible.

- The applicant should sign a statement indicating that the information provided is complete and accurate.

- The agency will send the form and the commissioning letter to the GP for completion of the health assessment.

Part C and procedure for the GP

- The GP must acknowledge that they have reviewed the information provided by the applicant and add any relevant comments or recommendations.

Adult health assessment

- The applicant's GP is requested to provide accurate and up-to-date information concerning any changes in pre-existing health issues, as well as details of any new health issues that have arisen since the last assessment. The applicant's GP is not required to make a decision on suitability but to provide sufficient accurate and detailed information to enable the medical adviser to advise the agency on health risk when considering the applicant's suitability to care for a child.
- The GP should complete the form, providing detailed information wherever relevant. The GP may wish to include relevant reports with the form when returning it to the agency medical adviser.

Interpretation of Form AH2 by the agency medical adviser

- The agency medical adviser should review all of the information provided by the applicant and their GP to determine if there has been a significant change in health that would warrant obtaining further information from consultants, or if health risk has altered, and should advise the agency accordingly.
- The guidance relating to Form AH is also applicable here.

Form AH Review

This form is under development by the CoramBAAF Health Group Advisory Committee.*

---

* Information about any new forms will be publicised via *CoramBAAF News*.

9 Additional resources

Further information on statute and guidance, and specific health issues in fostering and adoption, may be obtained at www.corambaaf.org.uk and from the publications listed in the bibliography.

Kent UASC health needs

Kent has had an unprecedented number of refugee children arrive in the last few years and the local authority's learning and resources are shared at www.uaschealth.org.

National UASC Transfer Protocol

This protocol, agreed by the DfES, Home Office, ADCS and Local Government Association, sets out the agreed roles and responsibilities for local authorities, central and regional administration teams and is available at: http://adcs.org.uk/safeguarding/article/national-uasc-transfer-protocol.

Royal College of Paediatrics and Child Health

This website supports paediatricians in the assessment and management of children and young people of refugee background and is available at: www.rcpch.ac.uk/improving-child-health/child-protection/refugee-and-unaccompanied-asylum-seeking-cyp/refugee-and-una.

Wessex Refugee Resource

This online resource, aimed at physicians in both primary and secondary care, provides links to Government guidelines and country-specific information for the countries of origin of refugee children and is available at: www.wessexrefugeeresource.com.

World Health Organisation

The World Health Organisation (WHO) provides data on international immunisation schedules and uptake rates past and present at www.who.int/immunization/monitoring_surveillance/data/en/. WHO also provides information about hepatitis B at www.who.int/mediacentre/factsheets/fs204/en/. WHO provides information about HIV/AIDS at www.who.int/gho/hiv/en/.

Bibliography

BAAF (2004) *Health Screening of Children Adopted from Abroad*, Practice Note 46, London: BAAF

BAAF (2006) *Genetic Testing and Adoption*, Practice Note 50, London: BAAF

BAAF (2007) *Reducing the Risk of Environmental Tobacco Smoke for Looked After Children and their Carers*, Practice Note 51, London: BAAF

BAAF (2008) *Guidelines for the Testing of Looked After Children who are at Risk of a Blood-Borne Infection*, Practice Note 53, London: BAAF

BAAF and BSHG (2011) *Statement on the Use of DNA Testing to Determine Racial Background*, London: BAAF

CoramBAAF (2015a) *Carer-Held Health Record*, London: CoramBAAF

CoramBAAF (2015b) *The Provision of Information to Fostering for Adoption Carers*, Practice Note 59, London: CoramBAAF

Department for Education (2005a) *Special Guardianship Regulations 2005*, London: DfE

Department for Education (2005b) *Adoption Agencies Regulations 2005*, London: DfE

Department for Education (2010) *Care Planning, Placement and Case Review (England) Regulations 2010*, London: DfE

Department for Education (2011a) *Information Sharing: How to judge a child or young person's capacity to give consent*, available at: http://media.education.gov.uk/assets/files/pdf/h/how%20to%20judge%20capacity%20to%20give%20consent.pdf

Department for Education (2011b) *Fostering Services Regulations 2011*, London: DfE

Department for Education (2011c) *Adoption Agencies and Independent Review of Determinations (Amendment) Regulations 2011*, London: DfE

Department for Education and Department of Health (2015) *Promoting the Health and Well-Being of Looked After Children*, London: DfE and DH

DHSSPS (1989) *Adoption Agencies Regulations (Northern Ireland) 1989*, Belfast: DHSSPS

DHSSPS (1995) *Children Order 1995 Guidance and Regulations, Volume 3: Family Placements and Private Fostering (Northern Ireland)*, Belfast: DHSSPS

DHSSPS (1996) *Arrangements for Placement of Children (General) Regulations (Northern Ireland)*, Belfast: DHSSPS

Goodman R (1997) 'The Strengths and Difficulties Questionnaire: a research note', *Journal of Child Psychology and Psychiatry*, 38, pp 581–586

Graham-Ray L (2015) *The Story So Far: Stories from our looked after children and care leavers*, London: Central London Community Healthcare NHS Trust

HM Government (2015) *Information Sharing: Advice for practitioners providing safeguarding services to children, young people, parents and carers*, available at https://www.gov.uk/government/publications/safeguarding-practitioners-information-sharing-advice

Lord J and Cullen D (2016) *Effective Adoption Panels: Guidance on regulations, process and good practice in adoption and permanence panels*, London: CoramBAAF

Mather M and Lehrer K (2010) *Evaluating Obesity in Substitute Carers*, London: BAAF

Meltzer H, Corbin T, Gatward R, Goodman R and Ford T (2003) *The Mental Health of Young People Looked After by Local Authorities in England*, London: Stationery Office, available at: www.ons.gov.uk/ the-mental-health-of-young-people-looked-after

Merredew F and Sampeys C (eds) (2015) *Promoting the Health of Children in Public Care: The essential guide for health and social work professionals and commissioners*, London: BAAF

Millar I with Fursland E (2006) *A Guide for Medical Advisers: Scotland*, London: BAAF

Monitor and NHS England (2016a) *National Tariff Payment System 2016/17*, London: Monitor and NHS England

Monitor and NHS England (2016b) *National Tariff Payment System 2016/17: Annex B: Technical guidance and information for services with national currencies*, London: Monitor and NHS England

Plumtree A (2014) *Child Care Law: A summary of the law in Scotland*, London: BAAF

Royal College of Paediatrics and Child Health and Royal College of Nursing (2015) *Looked After Children: Knowledge, skills and competences of health care staff – Intercollegiate role framework*, London: RCPCH

Scottish Government (2009a) *Adoption Agencies (Scotland) Regulations 2009*, Edinburgh: Scottish Government

Scottish Government (2009b) *Adoption (Disclosure of Information and Medical Information about Natural Parents) (Scotland) Regulations 2009*, Edinburgh: Scottish Government

Scottish Government (2009c) *Looked After Children (Scotland) Regulations 2009*, Edinburgh: Scottish Government

Scottish Government (2011) *Guidance on the Looked After Children (Scotland) Regulations 2009 and the Adoption and Children (Scotland) Act 2007*, Edinburgh: Scottish Government

Bibliography

Scottish Government (2012) *National Guidance for Child Protection in Scotland: Guidance for health professionals in Scotland*, available at: www.gov.scot/Publications/2012/12/9727

Scottish Government (2014) *Guidance on Health Assessments for Looked After Children and Young People in Scotland*, Edinburgh: Scottish Government

Welsh Government (2003) *Fostering Services (Wales) Regulations 2003*, Cardiff: Welsh Government

Welsh Government (2005) *Adoption Agencies (Wales) Regulations 2005*, Cardiff: Welsh Government

Welsh Government (2015) *Care Planning, Placement and Case Review (Wales) Regulations 2015*, Cardiff: Welsh Government

Appendix: CoramBAAF health forms

The CoramBAAF health forms can be viewed in the members' area of the CoramBAAF website by employees of agencies that are CoramBAAF members, or by individual/associate members – visit www.corambaaf.org.uk. If you are not a member, email pubs.sales@corambaaf.org.uk to be sent sample copies of the forms.

All of the forms are available electronically via the licence scheme. Agencies can purchase a Licence Agreement that gives them permission to use the form on their IT network. CoramBAAF supplies Microsoft Word templates of all the forms licensed. For further details, contact the Publications Department on 020 7520 7517 or email pubs.sales@corambaaf.org.uk. In addition, Forms AH and AH2 can be purchased in hard copy.

The CoramBAAF health forms are valid UK-wide.

Form AH

Comprehensive health report on prospective applicant for fostering/adoption/intercountry adoption/special guardianship/short break/respite care/kinship care/other care.

Form AH2 (update of Form AH)

Update adult health report from records

Consent Form

Consent form for obtaining and sharing of health information on child and birth parent.

Form M

Obstetric report on mother.

Form B

Neonatal report on child.

Appendix: CoramBAAF health forms

Form PH

Report on health of birth parent.

Form IHA–C

Initial health assessment for child from birth to nine years.

Form IHA–YP

Initial health assessment for young person 10 years and older.

Form RHA–C

Review health assessment for child from birth to nine years.

Form RHA–YP

Review health assessment for young person 10 years and older.

Form CR–C

Carers' report – profile of behavioural and emotional well-being of child from birth to nine years.

Form CR–YP

Carers' report – profile of behavioural and emotional well-being of young person aged 10–16 years.

Promoting the health of children in public care –
The essential guide for health and social work professionals and commissioners

Promoting the health of children in public care

THE **ESSENTIAL GUIDE** FOR HEALTH AND SOCIAL WORK PROFESSIONALS AND COMMISSIONERS

Edited by
Florence Merredew
and Carolyn Sampeys

BAAF
ADOPTION & FOSTERING

£19.95

306pp   235x170mm   ISBN 978 1 910039 26 7

With contributions from experienced medical and social work practitioners, this guide provides comprehensive advice on all aspects of the health of looked after and adopted children and their families, along with summaries of the relevant legislation, regulations and guidance. Individual chapters follow a child's journey through care and include information on: the health of looked after children, including mental health and well-being; pathways through care and issues of consent; the particular needs of groups of vulnerable children, including black and minority ethnic children, unaccompanied asylum-seeking children, those who are privately fostered or adopted from overseas, and care leavers; the assessment of adult carers, and common health concerns; confidentiality, information sharing and management of health records; and quality assurance, audit, clinical governance and commissioning.

Available from www.corambaaf.org.uk/bookshop